Not Another Dating Book is ... someone who is intentionally ... a blessing for singles who are serious about finding God's will for their dating lives and the kind of book I wish had been around when I was "lookin' for love" in all the wrong places!"

—**Kerri Pomarolli**, author of
Guys Like Girls Named Jennie? And *How to Ruin Your Dating Life*

As someone who reaches out to women in their twenties, I truly appreciate Renee Fisher's passion and candor in *Not Another Dating Book*. Within the devotions, the reader will catch the fire of Renee's passionate faith and rethink their perceptions about relationships. It's tough to find raw and relevant books on godly relationships, but Renee does not disappoint. I'll be recommending this to all the twentysomething women in my life!

—**Sarah Martin**, www.liveitoutblog.com

Renee Fisher is a courageous and trusted voice for the twentysomething generation. A faithful servant and inspirational leader, Renee's points to God and encourages her peers to do the same. She speaks directly to young adults where they are, in language they understand, dealing with the issues that matter to create a book that will encourage you no matter what your relationship status.

—**Suzanne Physick**, www.DatingGod.net.

We live in a time when our college students don't give two cents' worth of time or attention to the church. It is more important today than ever before in history to grab the attention of this age group. I don't want to get to heaven, look at God, and say, "Well...they just didn't fit our demographic, so we didn't reach out to them." It's time for the church to wake up and realize the importance of capturing the hearts of our young adults. I really believe that Renee Fisher has that vision and heart.

—**Blake Bergstrom,** Nashville Campus Pastor, Cross Point Church, Nashville

Not Another Dating Book is just that: not another "how to" book on the mysterious and frustrating but always soul-building work of dating. Renee's faith, passion, and struggle to be God's woman *now and not later* shines through in this book. Solid, honest, inspirational, and Biblical, this book is a welcomed addition to all those "other" dating books.

—**Jim Kane**, Pastor at First Church of God, Kendallville, Indiana

Renee Fisher has crafted a unique devotional that tackles core life issues rarely discussed from a biblical worldview. This is much-needed guidance for navigating the confusing world of dating—and an excellent resource for churches truly wanting to come alongside the new generation.

—**Lindy Lowry**, editor of *Outreach* magazine

In *Not Another Dating Book*, Renee Fisher takes devotions to the next level! The daily inspirations are full of golden nuggets and written with transparency, honesty, and integrity. If you want to grow in your human relationships, read this book.

—**Rob Tucker**, Pastor of Youth and Young Adults,
Living Word Community Church, York, Pennsylvania

Renee Fisher truly is a devotional master. Her authentic and practical writing style disarms the preconceptions you came with and you quickly find yourself laughing, sometimes wincing, and somehow unexpectedly engaging God in the process. It is a worthy read to help navigate that complicated arena of relationships.

—**Michael Forney**, Associate Pastor of
Gateway Church, Poulsbo, Washington

Like a best friend, Renee Fisher takes single Christians by the hand and sits down beside them. Just as the title suggests, this devotional is so much more than a dating book. Renee challenges twentysomethings to fall in love with God first. With thought-provoking questions and the truth of God's word, *Not Another Dating Book* should be on the nightstand of every Christian single who longs for the love of their life. Which I believe is just about every one of us.

—**Crystal Renaud**, author of *Dirty Girls Come Clean*

Renee brings back memories, asks the questions we all have, and directs us to draw closer to God in this book. She reminds us of the desire to love and build relationships in a godly and holy manner and helps us to laugh at the awful dating moments we've all experienced.

—**Chelsea Curley**, www.kugirl84.wordpress.com

You'll find charm and honesty, stories that will make you laugh out loud and some that might make you cry. You'll find an author who doesn't pull punches about the complicated intersections between romance and faith. And you'll find a message rooted in Scripture from beginning to end. If you want to know what the Bible says about relationships and what that means for you—dating or not—this book is a fantastic place to start.

—**Lisa Velthouse**, author of *Saving My First Kiss* and *Craving Grace*

Not Another Dating Book is a refreshing look at the complicated dating process. Packaged in an easy-to-read devotional format, it offers you one dating-related thought to focus on each day. I wish I'd had this book when I was single. It would have saved me a lot of heartache.

—**Shannon Primicerio**, author of *The Divine Dance*

Those of us deep in the dating world know it's important to be in God's word on a daily basis. This book is a good tool to lead you in that process. In the end you'll be closer to the Lord and better abe to recognize the man or woman of your dreams.

—**Megan Carson**, author of *A Year of Blind Dates*

Wow! A book about relationships that I don't want to laugh at or throw out my window! This book won't tell you what you should and shouldn't do. Rather it validates all the things we already feel and deal with in the world of dating, and encourages us along the way.

—**Christy Polek**, www.christypolek.com

Not Another Dating Book avoids stereotypical dating advice that only seems to work for two percent of the population. This is a book for the average people who are pursuing God and His will.

—**Dan Kimball**, author of *They Like Jesus but Not the Church*

If you are confused by what to think about dating, about singleness, about waiting…then Renee will provide you with straight-talking, grace-giving wisdom. Rather than pointing you just toward your future spouse, Renee points you to the only place of true life—a daily, growing relationship with God.

—**Nicole Unice**, author of *The Divine Pursuit*

Renee Fisher's *Not Another Dating Book* is an amalgam of proverbial wisdom and personal transparency. Diving in to this book is to dive it to an ocean where the water is so clear you can see the bottom of the earth's floor. You will not have to guess where she stands. You will not misunderstanding God's commands. If you are single, *you need this book*!

—**Tim Ross**, www.timross.org

If you're single and not interested in another dating book, you need to read this book. It's real, it's relevant, it's fresh, and it speaks the truth to a deceived generation.

—**Pete Wilson**, author of *Plan B*

Not Another Dating Book has ample supply of solid advice for anyone trying to navigate the complicated (but wonderful) world of relationships. Renee Fisher offers biblical wisdom and practical advice on dozens of topics like online dating, sexual temptation, purity, and the meaning of *Christianese* phrases like "unequally yoked." A fun and helpful read!

—**Brett McCracken**, author of *Hipster Christianity: When Church & Cool Collide*

You can count on Renee Fisher's devotionals to be straightforward, honest, and unvarnished. She'll make you smile, ponder, and maybe even cringe a time or two as you reflect on what God's Word has to say about your spiritual identity, relationships, and journey towards becoming like Christ.

—**Larry Osborne**, Senior Pastor of
North Coast Church, Vista, California

Honest, on-target, and fun, Renee Fisher has given us the gift of a book that is about a whole lot more than dating. Guided by the wisdom of being immersed in the Scriptures for years, she asks the tough questions and digs into the issues we deal with whether single, dating, or married.

—**Ed Cyzewski**, author of
Coffeehouse Theology: Reflecting on God in Everyday Life

not
another
dating
book

Renee Fisher

HARVEST HOUSE PUBLISHERS

EUGENE, OREGON

Cover by Koechel Peterson & Associates, Inc., Minneapolis, Minnesota

Photography courtesy of Thrive Photography

Back cover author photo © Laura Clines Photography

Published in association with the literary agency of Credo Communications, LLC, Grand Rapids, Michigan, www
.credocommunications.net.

NOT ANOTHER DATING BOOK
Copyright © 2012 by Renee Fisher
Published by Harvest House Publishers
Eugene, Oregon 97402
www.harvesthousepublishers.com

Library of Congress Cataloging-in-Publication Data
  Johnson, Renee.
  Not another dating book / Renee Johnson.
    p. cm.
  ISBN 978-0-7369-4535-6 (pbk.)
  ISBN 978-0-7369-4536-3 (eBook)
  1. Man-woman relationships—Religious aspects—Christianity—Meditations. I. Title.
  BT705.8.J64 2012
  241'.6765—dc22

                                                                                    2011016524

Printed in the United States of America

          12 13 14 15 16 17 18 19 20 / BP-NI / 10 9 8 7 6 5 4 3 2 1

To Marc. I love you.
Isaiah 34:16

Acknowledgments

To Jesus Christ—the most important relationship in my life! You are my one and only. Thank You for protecting my huge heart and all of my emotions. Without you, I wouldn't be able to write this book! I cannot believe how You have blessed me with the desires of my heart!

To my dad, mom, and brother, for supporting me through this process and for your unfailing love and wisdom. I cherish the time I spend with you all (including Pala the pit bull!).

To my mentor, Pam Farrel. Wthout you this book would not be possible. You are the number-one person I have to thank for introducing me to Harvest House. I cannot imagine where I would be without your guidance and support. I love you!

To Harvest House. Thank you for giving me the opportunity of a lifetime. To Bob Hawkins, Jr., LaRae Weikert, Barb Sherrill, Kathleen Kerr, Terry Glaspey, John Constance, Pat Mathis, Heather Green, Abby Van Wormer, and everyone else I have yet to meet. Thanks again for hooking me up with the best gig ever. I love you all. I am so indebted to you all for allowing me to encourage others in the area of relationships. May God bless *you* and *your* relationships as a result!

Thank you to my friends at Credo Communications, including my agent, Karen Neumair. Thanks for all your hard work! I am so grateful for you.

To Amy Marie and Amanda for your editing skillz!

To my best friends who have been there throughout the years—Jenn, Amy, Rachel, Brenda, Summer, and Amy Marie. Thanks for all your kind words, love, and support.

And to Amy Marie, for your friendship over the past year and your advice on boys. I don't know where I'd be without your love, thoughtfulness, and *big* heart. Keep on giving, girl. The world needs more of you.

contents

Foreword

I don't claim to be an expert in dating. I know there are people who come closer to that expertise because of all their dating experience. But when I was growing up in a conservative household, my parents told me dating was wrong. Hanging out with a boy one-on-one was a *big* no-no. And if I wanted a date to go later than 9:00? Don't even think about it.

When our family moved from the Midwest to California I was shocked at the cultural differences. None of my friends' parents forbid them to date! I remember sitting on the asphalt during Phys. Ed. talking about which boys the girls wanted to kiss. *Kiss?* I was mortified. Was I the only girl in junior high who hadn't kissed a boy?

But now, more than a decade later, my parents—these are the same parents who told me I couldn't date until I was 35—are asking me who I'm seeing, who I've had coffee with, and whether or not they can set me up with a friend's son. No. No. No. It's not as easy as they think to find the perfect man, settle down, get married, and pop out babies. First there's this series of coffee, lunch, dinner, and movie dates, and then *maybe* a guy will initiate the *relationship conversation*. Could it get any more confusing?

I know I'm not the only one who is fed up, scared, or frustrated with relationships. I've kissed a lot of guys. I've tried online dating, but nothing's felt right. Nothing's felt like forever. So where do I look for answers?

So many Christian dating books are written for the Christian virgin with no dating experience at all. To date or not to date—that is the question. But you and I both know that there are bigger questions out there in the dating scene, and bigger struggles.

- How do I stay pure?
- Will I be single forever?
- How do I honor God with my relationships?
- How do I deal with a breakup?

Those questions—and many more—are the focus of this devotional. Exploring relationships from the first crush to happily ever after, each devotion includes a prayer for the day, musings on that day's topic, quotations, further reading, and journal space to ponder your own questions.

Every relationship brings its own unique set of problems and concerns, and I hope that this book will get you asking the right questions and initiating the conversations that will get you moving past those issues and into greater adventures, with your dates and with God. Regardless of the circumstances, we need God for His wisdom, understanding, mercy, grace, forgiveness, and love. Before you read any further, though, I want to offer you a disclaimer: This is not a dating book. It is not a self-help book or a promise that "If you do what I did, God will bless you with a spouse." Trust me—I've tried reading other dating books to find my spouse, and if their formulas were foolproof I'd be married by now! This book isn't all about me. This is about questions and answers, about learning to be content in singleness, and about finding your identity in Christ.

I've been as honest, open, and transparent as I can be in this book. It's been a learning process for me, too, and I welcome your feedback. To share further about your experiences on dating and relationships go to http://www.notanotherdatingbook.com.

CRUSHED

You lust for what you don't have and are willing
to kill to get it…You wouldn't think of just asking
God for it, would you?…If all you want is your
own way, flirting with the world every chance you
get, you end up enemies of God and his way.

JAMES 4:2,4 MSG

When I was five I had a crush on Jake. A big one. I can remember hiding behind couches whenever he walked by because I was afraid he'd see me. When we got older, he started flirting with me. (When I say *flirt*, I mean he was a creep. That's how boys show they like you, I guess!) As a young girl, I longed to be pursued. I couldn't wait for a crush to like me back. And when I grew up, I craved the distraction from reality that a crush provided. I would fantasize about whichever boy I liked.

There's something about a crush that makes me feel alive and beautiful. When I'm in between relationships—no crush in sight—I start to feel lonely, as if singleness is entirely *my* fault. I start to believe the lies that I'm not smart or pretty enough. There have been times when I allowed a crush to distract me from the things God had for me instead of giving my longings to Him. I forced the crush. I rushed. Pushed harder. I wanted to initiate instead of waiting for the guy to pursue me.

But our job is to trust God and wait on His timing. Instead of panicking when I don't have a crush as a constant distraction, I choose to spend time with God and find my fulfillment in Him. A crush shouldn't distract you from your relationship with God—it should bring you closer. In Romans 4, Paul says that Abraham never wavered in believing God's promise. "In fact, his faith grew stronger, and in this he brought glory to God" (Romans 4:20). Will you hold on to the promise too—even when He seems farthest away? Remember—His timing is perfect!

Dear Jesus,

It's amazing that You care about my relationships—even the crushes! Help me to honor You when I have a crush, and not be distracted from my worship of You. Keep me from lust, and, when I'm lonely or frustrated, show me that You are more than enough. Amen.

Read Romans 4:20-21 and write a thank-you note to God below for His promises.

_____

_____

_____

_____

_____

_____

_____

_____

_____

_____

"How is it that you can find a woman attractive or beautiful, but not feel a spark or chemistry with her?"—*Meghan, 32*

Run!

Kiss me and kiss me again, for your
love is sweeter than wine.

Song of Solomon 1:2

I recently spoke on purity to a number of groups of teens and pre-teens at schools in Southern California. It didn't surprise me how curious the girls were about relationships. "When is it okay to kiss a boy?" they asked. "How do I get a guy to notice me?" "Is it appropriate to talk to him outside of school? Where? For how long?" Questions like this brought me back to the time when my dad sat me down and told me, "No dating until you're 35!" I thought he was being overprotective, overbearing—but was he? Even though he was only joking, my father understood my need for constant affection. I had my first kiss when I was nineteen and it changed the relationship really fast—too fast. The guy went from crush to boyfriend to saying "I love you" in three weeks. It freaked me out and I broke up with him.

The Bible doesn't ever say, "Thou shalt or shalt not date." It is pretty clear when it comes to setting appropriate physical boundaries, however. One passage says "there must not be even a hint of sexual immorality" in your life (Ephesians 5:3 NIV), and another says, "Run from sexual sin!" (1 Corinthians 6:18). Then how on earth are you supposed to be in the same room as your crush? Once the physical component is introduced into a relationship, I feel like I can't get enough. I think if I just kiss him he'll like me, and then we'll be together forever.

Is your relationship or that crush you can't get out of your mind more about the physical than growing together as a couple? *Run.* Is it just about meeting up for the next make-out session? Sure, that meets a need now—but what about in the long run? When we give in to temptation it takes absolute control of us. I've seen ungodly relationships become the number-one factor in my friends' decisions to leave the church altogether. Running from temptation when it first arrives will save much greater heartache in the future.

Dear Jesus,

Show me my limit. Show me where to draw the line and help me stay focused on the boundaries at all times—especially when I don't want to. Teach me why they're important. Thank You for Your grace, mercy, and love. Amen.

Read 1 Corinthians 10:12-13. Are you being tempted? How is God showing you a way out?

_____

_____

_____

_____

_____

_____

_____

_____

"A crush is so important to growing up and learning about life and love. The flutters in the tummy, the sweaty hands, the nerves…It can be exciting if that someone returns the crush and can be devastating if they don't. But all in all, you can learn a lot from those little butterflies."—*Amanda, 24*

Transformed

> When the woman realized that she could not
> stay hidden, she began to tremble and fell to her
> knees before him. The whole crowd heard her
> explain why she had touched him and that she had
> been immediately healed. "Daughter," he said to
> her, "your faith has made you well. Go in peace."

LUKE 8:47-48

Everybody likes a happy ending. We all crave a power like the woman in this story felt—a power greater than ourselves that can restore us to wholeness. That was the power that left Jesus's body when the woman who had been ill for so many years touched Him. Doctors had given up on her, and she had lost all hope. Until this man Jesus showed up.

She was too embarrassed or afraid to be seen, so she just reached out when she thought no one was paying attention and touched His robe.

But Jesus was paying attention. He knew that someone had touched Him. He knew He had the power to transform not just the woman's disease-ridden body, but also her heart. That's why He called her out in front of everyone. "When the woman realized that she could not stay hidden, she began to tremble," Luke says.

How often is that like us? We feel totally and completely unsatisfied. We long for...*someone*. We dare to dream of the day when that guy or girl is going to walk into the room and change our lives forever. But what happens when he or she does? What if those feelings of unworthiness (like the woman felt) don't go away? What if it turns out that a human being won't be able to satisfy all the longings of our hearts? Let Jesus heal, fulfill, and transform your heart, the same way He fulfilled and transformed the woman who came to Him.

Dear Jesus,

You see me. You hear all my prayers. You see me when I'm lying in bed at night crying and feeling alone. You see me when I'm at work or school, waiting to be noticed. Thank You, Holy Spirit, that Your love never fails and Your grace is unending. Help me to apply it to my relationships as I wait in eager anticipation for my own happy ending. Amen.

Read Luke 8:40-48. Are you currently coping without hope? How will you allow Jesus to transform you today?

_____

_____

_____

_____

_____

_____

_____

_____

_____

_____

"Right now I am in the beginning stages of a relationship. I would say I'm mostly happy with this, but I am a little frustrated that he is dragging his feet on making things official."—*Jeanna, 27*

Temporary and Eternal

See how very much our Father loves us, for he calls
us his children, and that is what we are! But the
people who belong to this world don't recognize that
we are God's children because they don't know him.

1 JOHN 3:1

One of my roommates has never been kissed. She's a beautiful woman, and it's not like she's never had the opportunity. She says that guys have tried to kiss her, but she never felt that spark. She never felt chemistry. She wants to be more than a friend with benefits, and so she keeps the friendship platonic. She's saving her first kiss for the guy who will blow her away. She's looking for a guy who will be there for her forever, and she refuses to give the gift of her first kiss to someone less than worthy. She hears our culture and media telling her she isn't normal or healthy and decides to reject those lies. I wish I could bottle her courage and give it away with this book!

How often do we look for temporary satisfaction instead of eternal? Do we have so little faith in the assurance of God's promises? In Ephesians 3:20 Paul cries out in praise, saying, "Now all glory to God, who is able, through his mighty power at work within us, to accomplish infinitely more than we might ask or think." No matter how He chooses to fulfill your desires, you can count on Him blowing you out of the water.

My roommate is waiting on God's timing. Are you? Dig into the Word and listen for His voice. That way, you'll be focused on eternal satisfaction and hear God's call loud and clear, no matter how many voices are trying to drown it out!

Dear Jesus,

Timing is everything. Help me to put Your thoughts above my needs. You know exactly what I need and when I need it, and I ask for patience as I wait for the man or woman You have planned for me! Amen.

Read 2 Corinthians 1:21-22. Do you feel that Christ has set you apart? For what purpose?

_____

_____

_____

_____

_____

_____

_____

_____

_____

"I look forward to the day when I'll be with a guy I'm interested in, but in the meantime that doesn't mean that I can't enjoy my singleness. I love my church running group and enjoy meeting guys who have mutual interests."—*Genevieve, 23*

THE FLIRT

Promise me, O women of Jerusalem,
by the gazelles and wild deer, not to
awaken love until the time is right.

SONG OF SONGS 2:7

It says three times in the Song of Solomon not to "awaken" love until the right time (2:7; 3:5; 8:4). And did you catch this part? Solomon says it to the *women*.

That's no coincidence. Women seem to know instinctively how to get a guy's attention. We know just how to walk, talk, and bat our eyelashes. In short, we know how to *flirt*. But we don't always know where to draw the line.

Flirting is fun. We all crave attention, and flirting seems like a harmless way to get it. It lets a person know you're interested. But have you noticed how easy it is to go too far? I know I've been in relationships that seem to go from zero to sixty in the matter of a few dates or weeks (whichever comes first).

We all need reminders, like this one in Song of Songs. Be careful not to let your flirting go too far, or before you know it you may have committed yourself farther than you're willing to go. Without meaning to, you might convince a guy that you're far more interested than you really are, setting him up for heartbreak and setting *yourself* up for a potentially dangerous—or at least a very *awkward*—situation. When you're flirting, remember that you may be holding another person's heart in your hands!

Dear Jesus,

Thank You for the incredible gift of communication, that we can use our voices and bodies to attract others. Help me to keep appropriate boundaries at home, school, or in the workplace. Amen.

Read Song of Songs 2:7. Where are your boundaries in flirting? How can you honor God through it?

_____

_____

_____

_____

_____

_____

_____

_____

_____

"I was standing and talking to this really cute guy, face-to-face and flirting (naturally). After a few minutes I realized that my fly was down. Epic fail." —*Danielle, 25*

THE NUMBERS GAME

People may cover their hatred with pleasant words, but they're deceiving you. They pretend to be kind, but don't believe them. Their hearts are full of many evils. While their hatred may be concealed by trickery, their wrongdoing will be exposed in public.

PROVERBS 26:24-26

So...how many people have *you* dated?

In some Christian communities, if you answer more than two or three you'll see some raised eyebrows. There's nothing wrong with dating, but remember: Playing the field should be left to a sporting event—not your love life. If you're looking for a series of brief, uncommitted relationships for satisfaction, you've got a problem. In Mark 7:21-22 Jesus says, "from within, out of a person's heart, come evil thoughts, sexual immorality...lustful desires...pride, and foolishness." How's your heart? Have you given it to more people than you can even name? Being single is hard, but it only gets harder when you decide to mess around with people to whom you haven't really made a commitment.

Everyone needs friends to keep them accountable. Friends who can be totally honest with each other, even when the truth is painful. God tells us to be holy and help each other out. "If another believer is overcome by some sin, you who are godly should gently and humbly help that person back onto the right path" (Galatians 6:1). Thank God for friends who can keep us from falling, and who help sustain us during the dry periods. A quick fling will never satisfy like these friendships, and an endless list of dates, no matter how large, can never compare to the abundance of God's love.

Dear Jesus,

*Show me how to protect myself from all kinds of trickery
and wrongdoing. Thank You for forgiving me of past sins and
renewing my soul through Your never-ending grace and love.
Amen.*

Read Galatians 6:7-10. What are you planting today that will reap an everlasting harvest?

_____

_____

_____

_____

_____

_____

_____

_____

"Why do we have to play games all
the time?"—*Suzanne, 29*

THE FRIEND ZONE

And we know that God causes everything to work
together for the good of those who love God and
are called according to his purpose for them.

ROMANS 8:28

Y ou're a really great person. Let's just be friends."
I hate that line. I hear those words and immediately regret all the
things I did to impress the guy saying them. The new haircut and high-
lights. The pedicures. The makeup. The cute dress. The matching shoes.
I wish I'd never done any of it...and I sure don't want to be his friend
anymore. What about you? Have you been there?

It hurts. And it's about that time that I don't want to believe in God's
goodness anymore. I don't want to believe that everything is working
together for my good. But the Bible says God doesn't withhold anything
from those who seek Him. "Keep on asking, and you will receive what
you ask for," Jesus says in Matthew 7:7.

Are you stuck in a moment, wishing for a relationship with someone
who's only interested in friendship? Pray about it. Not sure how to inter-
act with the coworker you can't take your eyes off of? Spend some time
getting wise council. Are you eyeing someone in your group of friends?
Go out of your way to show them who you are, but don't go over the top.
All too often, we get caught up in trying to impress the opposite sex and
end up wounding our pride...or committing our heart to a person who
won't keep it well. It's when our desire to impress others supersedes our
desire for God that we get ourselves into trouble. Big time. God is our
Living Water and Bread of Life. He is more than enough to supply all of
our needs—including our need for a relationship.

Dear Jesus,

Encourage and empower me to see beyond my disappointed hopes. Thank You for Your grace and mercy, and for the plans You are working out for my good. Amen.

Read Romans 8:25-28. What are your "groanings that cannot be expressed in words"? What would it take for you to give them over to God?

_____

_____

_____

_____

_____

_____

_____

_____

_____

"Once, in high school, I took a girl to a dance.
Once we got there she never talked or danced
with me. Lamest thing ever!"—*John, 21*

Desire

Stay away from fools, for you won't
find knowledge on their lips.

PROVERBS 14:7

He was tall. He was good-looking. He was—I've just got to say this—a really good kisser. He knew my faith was important to me and so he never pushed me to do anything I wasn't comfortable with or compromise my principles. But the thing was…he wasn't a Christian.

I heard today's verse in church one morning when I was seeing him and almost fell out of my chair. *I wouldn't find knowledge on his lips.* How did the pastor know what I was struggling with? Did God put him up to it?

Intimacy—even something as "innocent" as kissing—belongs in the context of a relationship. Becoming someone's friend-with-benefits can seem tempting in those moments when it seems that God will never say anything but *No,* but it's not what God intended for His children. God has so much better in store for you. He has plans to prosper you and not to harm you, and He wants to bless you beyond what you can ever dream up or imagine (Jeremiah 29:11; Ephesians 3:20).

An unhealthy friends-with-benefits relationship will cause you physical, emotional, and spiritual harm. The relationship can become like a drug. If gone unchecked, a simple make-out session with a friend can lead to sins that are even harder to control. James 1:15 says, "These desires give birth to sinful actions. And when sin is allowed to grow, it gives birth to death." I don't let my desires get in the way of God's best, because He "blesses those who patiently endure testing and temptation. Afterward they will receive the crown of life that God has promised to those who love him" (James 1:12).

Dear Jesus,

The entrapment I feel in my earthly body can be stifling. Remind me that every good and perfect gift comes from You alone, and keep me pure as a child of the King. Amen.

Read James 1:2-18. What trials and temptations are you enduring right now? What desires do you have that could "give birth to sinful actions"?

_____

_____

_____

_____

_____

_____

_____

_____

_____

"Friends-with-benefits almost never work. If you just want to fulfill a physical need, then you are overstepping God, telling Him that you are going to do things your way and not His way." —*Richard, 26*

GOOD NEWS TO THE BLIND

> Jesus told them, "Go back to John and tell
> him what you have heard and seen—the blind
> see, the lame walk, the lepers are cured, the
> deaf hear, the dead are raised to life, and the
> Good News is being preached to the poor."
>
> MATTHEW 11:4-5

When I speak at singles events, I like to ask the audience where they think the best places are to meet new people. The answers are never very surprising. Through friends, they say, or at church, at work, or online. When going on blind dates, it's best to keep your eyes open and know which questions to ask.

Is he or she lame? In Matthew 15:14, Jesus teaches us to "ignore [hypocrites]. They are blind guides leading the blind, and if one blind person guides another, they will both fall into a ditch." This person might talk the talk, but when you start to inquire about their friends, lifestyle, and previous relationships, you'll notice a lot of red flags going up.

Has he or she overcome their circumstances? Sometimes life deals you a rough hand, and although God permits suffering, He grieves with us and wants us to thrive in the good works He has planned (Ephesians 2:10).

Does this person possess a tenacious spirit? Has their attitude been positively or negatively affected because of their experiences?

Does he or she make you want to be a better person? Does this person spend time in the Word daily, pray for others, and show that they love the Lord by their actions? "Faith by itself isn't enough," says James 2:17. "Unless it produces good deeds, it is dead and useless."

Dear Jesus,

*Thank You for giving me the tools and the Scripture to help
me stay the path, not to veer to the right or to the left. Help me
keep from evil through all circumstances. Thank You for Your
divine protection. Amen.*

Read Colossians 3:17. When you're on a date, how do you represent
Christ?

_____

_____

_____

_____

_____

_____

_____

_____

"I met a guy on eHarmony. The date was so
uncomfortable—I had more chemistry with our
waiter! As the date was ending he looked at me
and said, 'So, how should we pursue this?' I told
him I wasn't interested."—*Chelsea, 26*

SO YOU THINK *your* DATE WAS BAD?

I was a junior in high school and over at my girlfriend's parents' house for a pre-dance dinner. They'd stuffed us with this four-course dinner, and then her mom came out with this giant cheesecake. I knew I couldn't eat another bite, but I forced myself to eat it anyway, just to be polite. I started feeling uncomfortable and got up from the table, but I couldn't get to the bathroom before I threw up all over their carpet.—*Ryan, 28*

My date was twenty minutes late for coffee, and when he finally showed up he sat down and started talking about his goals and plans for the future. He wanted to be a high school teacher in a small town in Iowa, he wanted at least six children, and he wanted his wife to be a stay-at-home mom. "What do you think?" he said. "You up for it?" I replied that I was hoping to have a career after college, and he shrugged, stood up, and left. —*Stephanie, 20*

For prom, my boyfriend and I were going on a double date with another couple. We all planned to meet at my boyfriend's house. I got out of the car and realized that the other girl was wearing the exact same dress I had on...and she looked way better in it. My boyfriend couldn't stop laughing.—*Kendra, 22*

I'd asked this guy out for coffee, and I thought he understood that it was a date. We met at a coffee shop on campus and were having a great conversation when he started to look all nervous and twitchy. He nodded over to the door, where another woman had just walked in. "I'm thinking of asking her out," he said. "What do you think?"—*Gillian, 25*

When I had my first boyfriend my sophomore year of high school, my mom made him come over to our house and meet him before he could take me out. That's understandable. But she also said I couldn't go out on a date with him unless my best friend could go along to make sure nothing "bad" happened. So my first ever date was me, my boyfriend, and my best friend. He talked to her more than he talked to me. It was awful. —*Jenna, 21*

It was my first date with this guy I'd liked forever. He took me to Olive Garden and ordered salad without dressing for us. I looked surprised, and he informed me that "Dressing's really fattening. I don't think you need it." —*Shelli, 28*

I suggested one of my favorite restaurants to my date. He ended up being allergic to something in his meal, and we ended the evening by going to the Emergency Room. —*Nicole, 21*

My girlfriend and I were having a romantic dinner, candles and everything, and I felt like it was the right time to tell her I was in love with her. "Um, I don't think I can say the same thing," she said. —*Rob, 28*

I was invited to play pool with my boyfriend and his best friend. I had never played pool, and I didn't know any of the rules. I wasn't paying attention, and I accidentally jabbed the pool stick right into my boyfriend's stomach. Hard. —*Jaylene, 25*

Represent

Whatever you say or do, do it as a
representative of the Lord Jesus.

COLOSSIANS 3:17

The number of people who find their dates online is growing. More than 20 million people have subscribed to online dating sites such as Match.com and eHarmony.com. Most people know someone who's tried to find love online, with varying amounts of success. It sure isn't easy to know if you'd get along with a person based on a profile and a picture! As you start communicating, you can give away a lot of yourself to someone who's essentially a stranger. But it's tough to meet quality men and women in real-life scenarios. All those 20 million people can't be wrong...right?

But some statistics are even more startling—especially if you're looking for a date who's committed to Christ. Studies vary, but most agree that large numbers of teens and young adults who were raised in the church—somewhere between 70 and 90 percent—end up leaving their faith behind. (Many of them will eventually find their way back into the church again, but our congregations are largely deprived of young adults.) Many young adults feel like the church isn't relevant anymore. They say the church isn't willing to discuss the hard issues, or it's not making a real difference in the community. For these twenty-somethings, Christianity is about legalism, not transformation.

The people you meet through online dating sites, work, or mutual friends, might be part of these statistics. The faith you hold might have negative connotations for them. How can you show them what it really means to follow Jesus? Will you be one more Christian who judges and condemns, or will you model the infinite love of Christ?

Dear Jesus,

You know my heart. You know my secret doubts and struggles. Answer those questions, Lord, and let me be a light to those around me—those who haven't truly seen Your face. Amen.

Read Colossians 3:1-17. What can people learn about Christ just by watching you?

_____

_____

_____

_____

_____

_____

_____

_____

_____

"Giving away the most intimate part of yourself won't bring the deep, meaningful connection that God has wired us to desire with your spouse. Each time you rationalize sex outside of marriage, it alters your belief system about relationships."—*Nicole, 38*

Deal Breakers

People who wink at wrong cause trouble,
but a bold reproof promotes peace.

PROVERBS 10:10

Do you just hate it when a guy blasts the music too loud when you're in his car? Or when a girl can't seem to tear herself away from texting and talking on her cell phone long enough to say hello? Maybe you'd never date someone who smokes, doesn't laugh at your jokes, or has a lot of baggage from a previous relationship. It's no question: Everyone has deal breakers in a relationship—beliefs we're not willing to compromise. But what does the Bible say our deal breakers should be?

Same spiritual beliefs. "Can two people walk together without agreeing on the direction?" (Amos 3:3). If a couple's beliefs are lopsided or unequal, they will never be able to grow together. Similarly, Paul warns us not to "team up with those who are unbelievers" (2 Corinthians 6:14).

Accepts authority. The Roman officer whose story is told in two Gospels had soldiers and slaves under his authority. He was a powerful man, and yet he accepted Christ's authority over him (Matthew 8:5-13). Does your date accept the roles God gave all of us? Does he respect those in authority? Does she accept God's authority over *her* life?

Hygiene habits. This isn't about how often your date flosses or what kind of deodorant he wears. It's about the state of his heart. Does he or she care more about the outward appearance than the inside? Beauty only scratches the surface of the skin. If your date's daily spiritual habits are as regular as a shower, you'll be able to see the fruit in his daily life.

Financially free. Can your date manage his or her pocketbook? Did she spend her rent money on a new pair of shoes? Did he blow his next paycheck on the latest toy? Scripture tells us to "Give to everyone what you owe them: Pay your taxes and government fees to those who collect them...Owe nothing to anyone—except for your obligation to love one another" (Romans 13:7-8).

All our deal breakers are different. Some of them won't really matter in the long run (he'll probably turn down his stereo when he has a baby in the backseat!), but don't compromise on a life partner whose heart isn't full of Christ.

Dear Jesus,

Thank You for being my guide in relationships. Help me to trust You while I wait for Your perfect timing. Amen.

Read 2 Corinthians 6:14-18. What are your deal breakers?

_____

_____

_____

_____

_____

_____

_____

_____

_____

"The first two things I look for in a man are (1) his love for Christ and (2) that his life is the product of repentance and grace."—*Lisa, 29*

RULES

So whether you eat or drink, or whatever
you do, do it all for the glory of God.

1 CORINTHIANS 10:31

It seems like relationships are all about rules, doesn't it? Casual dating isn't so casual anymore. There are hundreds of books on the market to tell you exactly what to do and not to do when you're trying to attract someone's attention—*The Rules: Time-Tested Secrets for Capturing the Heart of Mr. Right, The Complete Idiot's Guide to a Healthy Relationship,* and many, many more. "Do exactly what we tell you," these books proclaim, "and he'll put a ring on it!" If these books are true, there are rules about each one of these issues:

- Who makes the first move?
- Who decides where to meet? Public or private? Indoors or outdoors?
- What if he or she isn't on time?
- Who pays?
- How long do you wait for a call after the date is over?
- Should you send him or her a text on your way home? Or shoot them a Facebook message thanking them for the date? (That seems less threatening—right?)

I've had so many worries and concerns about which path to take and who to date that I couldn't even move forward! But check out what Paul says in 2 Corinthians 3:17: "For the Lord is the Spirit, and wherever the spirit of the Lord is, there is freedom." This was one of the hardest lessons for me to learn, but I've finally come to realize that I can't live my life by a series of rules. If it's not a sin issue, we have the freedom to choose, to decide, to fall flat on our faces and get up again. Christ will be with us through it all.

Dear Jesus,

Help me navigate the so-called rules of dating. Give me wisdom to make decisions that will lead me closer to You, and to have patience as You write my story. Thank You for Your love and support—no matter what. Amen.

Read Romans 6:14. What rules have you lived under? What does freedom in Christ look like for you?

_____

_____

_____

_____

_____

_____

_____

_____

_____

"I ask a girl out when I realize we have things in common and think that we'll have fun together."—*Tim, 26*

WHAT'S IN YOUR HEART?

The LORD looks at the heart.

1 SAMUEL 16:7

How are you supposed to "just know" when you meet the person you're going to spend your life with? Shouldn't there be a lot more analyzing and scrutinizing that goes into it? First dates always make me nervous for that very reason. Everything means something, right? If I'm smiling a lot, does that mean he's the one? Or does it mean I need to stop grinning like an idiot? Is there something in my teeth? And if I can't even figure *that* out, how do I know if I want to go on a second date?

Ask yourself if you have chemistry. Do you have interests in common? Does he make you laugh? Do you enjoy being around her? Does he share your passion for God, family, friends, and helping others? Remember what God told Samuel when he was looking for a new king to anoint for Israel: "Don't judge by his appearance or height…The LORD doesn't see things the way you see them. People judge by outward appearance, but the LORD looks at the heart" (1 Samuel 16:7). Before you go and judge someone's character or what's in his or her heart, spend some alone time with God. Ask Him what He sees in your heart.

The dating process can be exhausting. It will try and test your patience. Don't give up! Ask God to give you the gift of discernment as you seek the person who just might be "the one." And maybe, when God brings that man or woman into your life, your heart will match God's desire for you!

Dear Jesus,

Don't let my own sense of urgency or impatience get in the way as I pursue a new relationship. Help me to keep my thoughts and actions pure today and every day. Don't let me forget to guard my heart. Amen.

Read 2 Samuel 16:1-13. God speaks directly to Samuel when he points out David, the chosen king of Israel. Do you believe that God can still speak that clearly to your heart today?

_____

_____

_____

_____

_____

_____

_____

_____

_____

"It's the way she looks at me when I look at her that ropes me in for a second date. There should be a sparkle in her eyes. You might call it chemistry, but I would say it's an indicator of her sincerity and a playfulness that will spark romance further down the road." —*Logan, 29*

DEFINE YOUR RELATIONSHIP...
WITH CHRIST

Can two people walk together without
agreeing on the direction?

AMOS 3:3

Define The Relationship. A DTR is the conversation in which you and your date ask the tough questions. *Do we want to make this official? Where is this relationship heading?* It's a time to communicate expectations, hopes, and fears. It's never an easy conversation to have, but avoiding or putting off the DTR will only hurt your relationship.

If there's a problem in your relationship, or if you want a date to become more than a friend, the only way to resolve the issue is through communication. Listening to your boyfriend or girlfriend's concerns and sharing with him or her honestly is the only way to move forward.

It's the same with God. Before Jesus ascended to heaven, He said that God would "give [us] another Advocate, who will never leave [us]. He is the Holy Spirit, who leads into all truth" (John 14:16-17). We can communicate with the Spirit, telling God our hopes, dreams, fears, expectations, concerns, confusion, and doubts. We can speak in absolute honesty, trusting that nothing we say could ever separate us from Him or make Him love us any less. In his letter to the Romans Paul writes, "I am convinced that nothing can ever separate us from God's love. Neither death nor life, neither angels nor demons, neither our fears for today nor our worries about tomorrow—not even the powers of hell can separate us from God's love" (Romans 8:38). Jesus wants to have a close relationship with you—closer than any boyfriend or girlfriend, closer than any lover, closer than any husband or wife. The Bible is His love letter, calling you into deeper, stronger relationship—a relationship that will satisfy more than any earthly desire. Will you embrace Him today?

Dear Jesus,

I ask You for truth in my relationships. Help me decipher the mixed signals, lack of communication, or misplaced expectations. Thank You for Your help, even when the words may not come easily. I trust You. Amen.

Read John 14:15-17. Do you feel like you can speak openly with God? Do you feel that anything in your past could separate you from His love?

_____

_____

_____

_____

_____

_____

_____

_____

_____

"Besides pre-requisites (Christian, not-crazy, tall)
what is it that attracts a girl?"—*Paul, 21*

TO Have a Friend...

Imitate God, therefore, in everything you
do, because you are his dear children.

EPHESIANS 5:1

Two thousand years ago Paul wrote to Timothy, a young man he called his "true son in the faith" (1 Timothy 1:2), and challenged him to "Run from anything that stimulates youthful lusts. Instead, pursue righteous living, faithfulness, love, and peace. Enjoy the companionship of those who call on the Lord with pure hearts." Who wouldn't want to date someone like *that*?

One of the most important lessons I've learned is that I'll never find a relationship worth pursuing if I'm not already acting like a godly woman. If I'm hanging out in bars every weekend, I'll only meet people whose idea of a good time is...hanging out in bars. (And how can you really get to know someone in that kind of setting?) Are you acting like the kind of person you want to attract?

Check out what the apostle John says: "Let's not merely say that we love each other," he warns us. "Let us show the truth by our actions" (1 John 3:18). Did you get that? It's not just what we say, but what we *do* that matters to God. Are you looking for a responsible guy? Then start taking responsibility for your work today. Are you looking for a patient woman? Then start learning how to hold *your* tongue! Are you looking for someone who's gentle, devoted, forgiving, and committed to God? You can become that person too. And in the process, you'll be fulfilling Paul's instructions to the church in Ephesus. "Imitate God...in everything you do," he told them (Ephesians 5:1). Be Christ-like in your behavior, and you'll find yourself blessed beyond your wildest dreams.

Dear Jesus,

Help me to imitate You in everything I do, and to keep You always at the center of my relationships. Give me Your heart, Lord. Amen.

Read Ephesians 5:1-14. Which Christ-like qualities do you most need to imitate in your life? Which behaviors and attitudes need to be put aside?

_____

_____

_____

_____

_____

_____

_____

"No guy wants to date a nag. If you find yourself nagging, figure out why you are doing it and stop nagging—or stay single!" —*Lindsey, 31*

WHAT ARe you WeArInG?

Don't be concerned about the outward beauty of fancy
hairstyles, expensive jewelry, or beautiful clothes.

1 PETER 3:3

If you, like me, grew up in a legalistic household, today's passage meant exactly what it said. No makeup. Simple haircuts. No jewelry. Clothes from the outlet mall. I also suffered from severe eczema, at one point losing all the skin on my face. I thought I would never be beautiful again, and it took years for the Lord to heal me. I couldn't wear makeup because of my condition, but eventually I learned that I didn't need it. I was already beautiful—beautiful from the inside out. I couldn't rely on my outer beauty to attract attention. No, my self-confidence came from who I was as a whole person. King Solomon, the wisest man in the world, esteemed women this way: "Charm is deceptive, and beauty does not last; but a woman who fears the LORD will be greatly praised. Reward her for all she has done. Let her deeds publicly declare her praise" (Proverbs 31:30-31).

What makes a woman attractive to the opposite sex? Undress her down to what really matters, and she should clothe herself "with the beauty that comes from within" (1 Peter 3:4). God used scared teenagers, prostitutes, widows, and foreigners in His great plan to redeem the world. No matter how dark or light skinned, tall or short, skinny or curvaceous, God's message is clear: women matter!

Don't listen to the lies our society tells us about our hearts and our bodies. Learn to speak truth over your thoughts, and allow God to replace thoughts like "I intimidate guys," "I'm too fat," and "I'm not good enough" with "I'm passionate," "I love my body," and "His grace is enough."

Dear Jesus,

Every day I'm told that I need good looks and a solid relationship to be worth anything. Show me how to replace that lie with the truth—that I am Your beloved creation. Amen.

Read Romans 13:14 and Colossians 3:12. What kind of clothing makes a woman? What virtues have you been clothing yourself with?

_____

_____

_____

_____

_____

_____

_____

_____

_____

"High school and college girls are conditioned to not only look for and want relationships, but to *need* them! After getting out of a long relationship with the wrong guy, I prayed God would make me an independent girl who goes against the odds and can be totally fulfilled in her life without a boy!"—*Tabitha, 20*

Partners

Every time I think of you, I give thanks to my God.

PHILIPPIANS 1:3

At the beginning of his letter to the Philippians, Paul says, "Whenever I pray, I make my requests for all of you with joy, for you have been my partners in spreading the Good News about Christ from the time you first heard it until now." *Partners.* What a great way to think about a long-term relationship! Whether it's a couple just beginning their journey together or a husband and wife celebrating their golden anniversary, partners in life are facing the future together, committed to sharing each other's work, regrets, laughter, and sorrow. They'll be holding hands through thick and thin, ready to weather any storm.

This kind of partnership doesn't spring up overnight! It takes years of working and growing together, years of learning each other's strengths and weaknesses. And the relationship is planted rock solid in Jesus Christ. When people build their foundation on this rock, Jesus says, "Though the rain comes in torrents and the floodwaters rise and the winds beat against that house, it won't collapse because it is built on bedrock" (Matthew 7:25).

This partnership is a reflection, in fact, of Christ's relationship with *us.* Christ is ready to face all the troubles and trials of life right along with you. He wants to carry you and sustain you through the joy and through the times when you can barely hold up your head. "Give all your worries and cares to God, for he cares about you," says 1 Peter 5:7. Sounds like a partnership worth hanging on to!

Dear Jesus,

Help me remember to give thanks for the only true, lasting relationship there is—You! Thank You for meeting my needs and bringing the desires of my heart at the right time. Amen.

Read Philippians 1:1-11. What kind of partnership is Christ calling you to today?

_____

_____

_____

_____

_____

_____

_____

_____

"What do you think about and consider when deciding to make a commitment to another person?"—*Stacy, 25*

your First Love

But I have this complaint against you. You don't
love me or each other as you did at first!

REVELATION 2:4

I was 15 years old and spending a week of summer vacation in Colorado with Jake's family. My hair had grown out, my legs were long and thin, and my green eyes were sparkling. I was in love.

And so was Jake. He looked at me like he'd never seen me before. His gaze took my breath away. It would have been a week in paradise... except for one problem. My feet had broken out with eczema that year. It had spread over the tops of my feet and taken off all the skin. My feet were constantly wrapped up in bandages.

When we said good-bye, I crumbled. I didn't want to leave Jake. As I cried on the drive back home, the rash spread to my face and I lost all my skin. The pain hurled me into the arms of God, and I vowed to read the Word and learn more about my *first* love, God. It took me that entire year of reading through the Bible for the first time to see my pride. My catalyst came from Revelation 2:4-5: "But I have this complaint against you. You don't love me or each other as you did at first. Look how far you have fallen! Turn back to me and do the works you did at first."

I believed I loved Jake, but I was 15. What did I know? I let my emotions take control and I suffered. A lot. It took my body six years to recover from the flare-up of 1997. It wasn't until I spent time in the Word that I was able to see my mistake of thinking God couldn't love me as much as Jake did. Thankfully, God has spent the past 13 years proving me wrong! His love is ultimate. "Such love has no fear, because perfect love expels all fear" (1 John 4:18).

Dear Jesus,

Help me receive Your love when I have no more earthly love to give. Embrace me where I am and pour Your unchanging love into my stony heart. Amen.

Read Revelation 2:4-5. Have you allowed anyone to replace God as your first love?

_____

_____

_____

_____

_____

_____

_____

_____

_____

"Have I *ever* been through the pain of loving and losing someone! It was way back in high school but the pain still haunts me at times, even 12 years later."—*Christie, 27*

SO YOU THINK
your DATE WAS BAD?

I was going to prom with a whole group of friends. I had the biggest car, so I drove. I dropped all the girls off in front of the building and then went to park. I was waving to my girlfriend and not paying attention, and I rear-ended a limo. —*Jeff, 27*

I met a guy from eHarmony at a park in our neighborhood. He talked about himself the *whole time*. I couldn't get a single word in edgewise. Finally, after forty-five minutes, he said "Well, is there anything else you want to know about me?" No thanks, I'm good. —*Michelle, 25*

I got an out-of-the-blue phone call from a guy I barely remembered from high school asking me out to coffee. I figured I might as well. When I asked what he'd been up to for the past few years he said "Oh, I've been collecting every season of *Full House*. I've got them pretty much memorized now." —*Sara, 25*

I went on a date with a guy who ended up dining and dashing. I was sitting at the table waiting for him while he went to the "restroom"…and then I looked out the window to see him outside the restaurant waving at me, signaling me to run out and leave! I ended up paying for the entire meal myself. —*Christine, 28*

I went over to my date's house to pick her up for a dance. She got in the car and I proceeded to try to back out of the driveway with the emergency brake still on. Her parents, grandparents, and siblings were all standing there laughing. —*Ethan, 20*

I once asked a girl out from my church. I was super nervous, so the night before the date I scouted out the location and all the directions. Everything went well on the date, and I was so caught up in the conversation on the way home that I didn't realize I turned onto the off ramp of a highway. She started screaming, and cars were coming at us head-on. It was a miracle we weren't killed…but maybe not so surprising that we didn't go on a second date. —*Daniel, 32*

My ex-girlfriend had just broken up with me, but couldn't find a new date to her homecoming dance. Her mother called my mother, and my mom forced me to take her. It was awful. —*Nathan, 28*

My boyfriend took me for a picnic in the park after it had gotten dark, not realizing that it was illegal to be there after sunset. He'd just leaned over to kiss me when a policeman showed up and demanded to know what we were doing. —*Emily, 21*

LONG DISTANCE

The faithful love of the LORD never ends! His
mercies never cease. Great is his faithfulness;
his mercies begin afresh each morning.

LAMENTATIONS 3:22-23

I lived in California. Jake didn't. But what did that matter? When he
came back into my life six years after I first fell for him, I knew he
was my dream guy. My soul mate. I was certain that God intended us to
be together.

And at first it was great. Jake flew out to California, and we vowed to
make it work. I didn't doubt our relationship even for a second. Unfor-
tunately, I didn't know what I was getting myself into. He wasn't much
for communication, and I was the *over*-communicator. We didn't match.

We flew back and forth for a year, but after thousands of dollars and
untold numbers of long-distance phone calls, our relationship was over.
The breakup conversation only took four minutes! I was devastated, but
I knew better than to cry this time. I harbored bitterness towards God,
Jake, and myself for believing it was a done deal. It took me a long time
to get my relationship with God back on track, but I finally figured it out.
His mercies are new *every* morning. Gone was the mentality of thinking
I had everything figured out. My life and my future were in God's hands.

Have you ever felt like you and God are in a long-distance relationship? That you haven't seen each other for a while, and maybe you've
gotten off track? Maybe the communication isn't as good as it once was,
and you're too busy with the rest of your life to give Him a call at the
end of the day. "I have this complaint against you. You don't love me or
each other as you did at first," the Lord says in Revelation 2:4. Building
a relationship is a daily process, and God is *always* reaching out for you.

"My righteousness draws near speedily, my salvation is on the way...look to me and wait in hope" (Isaiah 51:5). Will you draw near to Him today?

Dear Jesus,

I always think I can make it work on my own, but even with the best of intentions I always fall short. Help me to not be wise in my own eyes, and make my relationships right today! Amen.

Read Lamentations 3:22-32. Have you ever felt "abandoned by the Lord"? How did you make your "long-distance relationship" with Him work?

_____

_____

_____

_____

_____

_____

_____

_____

_____

"I'm working on the whole forgiveness thing. I
have a hard time forgiving when the person won't
admit he's done anything wrong."—*Katrina, 24*

THE SPIRIT'S NUDGING

And I will give you a new heart, and I will put a new
spirit in you. I will take out your stony, stubborn
heart and give you a tender, responsive heart.

EZEKIEL 36:26

When I meet a guy, I'm always the one calling, texting, sending Facebook messages, making plans, and posting cute updates about our times together. And it feels like every one of these relationships ends in "Let's just be friends."

But I started to hear that inner voice nudging me, saying "It's not him. It's you." I've had to reexamine the way I work in relationships. I've always made it too easy for a date to get to know me. Once the mystery is gone, so is the guy. And when I really need a friend, I can't count on him to be there. It took a lot of getting my heart smashed into pieces before I was forced to put an end to these bad habits. No more changing a guy to fit my mold. That was the Holy Spirit's job. My role was to respond and wait!

In the Gospel of John, Jesus says, "The Spirit alone gives eternal life. Human effort accomplishes nothing. And the very words I have spoken to you are spirit and life" (John 6:63). When we listen to the flesh, we will give in to the enemy's attacks and succumb to temptation of the flesh. But when we live the words of Christ and apply them to our lives, we are promised new life. When we listen to the Spirit's urging—that little inner voice, nudging us to become better than we could be alone—we can be certain of receiving Christ's healing and restoration.

Dear Jesus,

Teach me how to be secure in my relationship with You first. Don't let me compromise the way You taught me to live just so that I can be in a relationship. Help me to recognize the Spirit's voice when He speaks in my heart. Amen.

Read Ezekiel 36:25-27. What is one thing about yourself you wish you could change? Ask God to give you a new understanding.

_____

_____

_____

_____

_____

_____

_____

_____

"I am constantly looking around at the guys, seeing if there is anyone that I could connect with, or asking myself why the guys I like don't like me."—*Danielle, 22*

GODLY JEALOUSY

You must worship no other gods, for the LORD,
whose very name is Jealous, is a God who
is jealous about his relationship with you.

EXODUS 34:14

I want to start out today by taking a look at Solomon. He was the wisest man who ever lived, but he wasn't always obedient. Check out this story from 1 Kings: "Now King Solomon loved many foreign women. Besides Pharaoh's daughter, he married women from Moab, Ammon, Edom, Sidon, and from among the Hittites. The LORD had clearly instructed the people of Israel, 'You must not marry them, because they will turn your hearts to their gods.' Yet Solomon insisted on loving them anyway. He had 700 wives of royal birth and 300 concubines. And in fact, they did turn his heart away from the LORD" (1 Kings 11:1-3).

Seven hundred wives...not even counting the concubines! In the end, they convinced Solomon to worship other gods and idols. Even though he knew better, he still chose not to obey God's command.

When you give your heart to someone, you want all of them. You want his or her mind, body, and heart as completely as you've given yourself. That's a godly jealousy, and that's why it hurts so much when your affections aren't returned, or when your ex starts seeing someone else. You offered all of yourself and had it thrown back in your face.

That's exactly how God feels about us. He was in a relationship with Solomon. He honored and blessed him with wisdom beyond compare. He "had appeared to him twice" (1 Kings 11:9). And what did Solomon do? He threw those blessings right back in God's face, building pagan shrines and offering sacrifices to idols.

What sacrifices have you made to other gods? What shrines have you built to the idols of materialism, lust, achievement, and reputation? God is jealous. He gave you all of Himself—He gave you His own Son! Turn back to Him today.

Dear Jesus,

I give my heart to You. You are jealous of my time, my affections, and my heart. Help me to give it back to You, because You are worth everything to me! Amen.

Read 1 Corinthians 1:1-22. What are your idols? How are they keeping you from a deeper relationship with God?

_____

_____

_____

_____

_____

_____

_____

_____

"I've definitely struggled with jealousy. My boyfriend dated a lot of people before me, and it used to bother me when he talked about his exes."—*Ashley, 34*

Free

The LORD's light penetrates the human
spirit, exposing every hidden motive.

PROVERBS 20:27

We all have a past. Things we've said or done that could affect our new relationships. Maybe you've slept around or maybe you've never been kissed. Maybe you're somewhere in the middle. But we all have doubts about ways our history could change our future.

Honesty is so crucial to a strong relationship. And not just honesty about the "big" stuff, like your past relationships. Be honest about your future. Be honest about your weaknesses. Be honest about your hopes, your regrets, and your fears. Honesty up front will prevent heartbreak later.

If you are hiding something, it will eventually be brought into the light. Maintain trust in your relationship by telling the truth and keep short accounts with each other. Don't let fear rule your relationships—whether it's a fear of the past coming back to haunt you, a fear of the unknown, or a fear of exposing your true self.

There's one Person who already knows the dark secrets of your past, of course. Someone who knows all your shame and has taken it onto Himself. Someone who knows the true self you keep hidden from the world, and who loves you anyway. "I have loved you, my people, with an everlasting love. With unfailing love I have drawn you to myself" (Jeremiah 31:3). The life Christ offers you has no room for shame, fear, or dishonesty. No—in Christ you are totally, unashamedly free.

Dear Jesus,

Holy Spirit, please guard my life. Don't let me follow the cravings of my sinful nature, but help me give myself to You, totally and unashamedly. Amen.

Read Proverbs 20:27. What secrets have you been keeping from those closest to you? What secrets have you been keeping from God?

_____

_____

_____

_____

_____

_____

_____

_____

_____

"Do women think it's okay for their boyfriends to
have close friends who are girls?"—*Peter, 20*

WHEN IT'S OVER

"Yes, I am the vine; you are the branches. Those
who remain in me, and I in them, will produce
much fruit. For apart from me you can do nothing."

JOHN 15:5

Have you ever written a letter to someone but then thrown it away
or burned it? Maybe you're like me, rehearsing your words to the
other person in front of the mirror. Or maybe you were taken completely
by surprise when the person who meant the most to you in the world
said, "This just isn't working for me."

No matter how you go about it, breakups are tough. Some are unex-
pected, and others we see a long time coming. After a painful breakup
we think it's over. There won't be any more chances at happiness. There
will never be a new relationship—someone else to make our eyes shine.
We whine. We cry. We go backwards. We want to be back with our ex, and
in the next breath we *hate* our ex. We do anything but glorify God with
our actions. It's as if we've taken our grace, crumpled it up, and thrown
it back in God's face. We sever trust and choose to dwell in our misery.

The Bible says, "You say you have faith, for you believe that there is
one God. Good for you! Even the demons believe this, and they tremble
in terror" (James 2:19). *Good job.* You believe…and now the tough part
remains. No matter how physically, verbally, or emotionally upsetting
a breakup is, we must remain in God. Our words, our actions, and our
every choice must be centered on God's will, not our own pain. Trust in
God's ability to write a happy ending for your story, no matter how much
trial you endure along the way. Remain. Remain. Remain.

Dear Jesus,

Relationships are sometimes too hot to handle, and my emotions can be all over the place. They drive me crazy and I can't think straight. This is why I need You now, today, more than ever. Amen.

Read John 15:1-8. Have you felt the sting of a broken relationship? What has it taught you about remaining in God?

_____

_____

_____

_____

_____

_____

_____

_____

_____

"When I was dating this guy the ex-girlfriend would always call right in the middle of a sentimental or romantic moment. It was seriously annoying."—*Amber, 29*

As We Forgive

Fire goes out without wood, and quarrels
disappear when gossip stops.

PROVERBS 26:20

Walk down any supermarket check-out lane and all you'll see is celebrity gossip. Who got married, who's sleeping around, and who's in the middle of a nasty divorce. It isn't pretty, and journalists dissect every bitter argument, every legal fight, and every cruel half-truth.

How do you react when *you're* the one with a broken relationship? Do you badmouth an ex-boyfriend? Do you take revenge on a woman you used to love? Juicy gossip goes a long way, especially with all the social media forums you have at your fingertips. Are you giving your pain and bitterness to God, or are you relishing it, channeling it into words designed only to hurt?

Check out what the apostle John says in 1 John 2:9: "If anyone claims, 'I am living in the light,' but hates a Christian brother or sister, that person is still living in darkness." *Ouch*. And in James 3:6, we're cautioned that "the tongue is a flame of fire. It is a whole world of wickedness, corrupting your entire body. It can set your whole life on fire, for it is set on fire by hell itself." So what's a broken, angry person to do?

Sounds like you're supposed to *love* your ex as a fellow Christian. It's good for them, and it's good for you. But how exactly do you love someone who's broken your heart? Do you run in fear and never talk to them again? Avoid all social situations and find a new group of friends ASAP?

Christians are called to something bigger than that. We're called to forgiveness. Although we may never forget the pain of the past, we can still find release from the vicious cycle of pain, bitterness, and anger. Will you ask God for the strength to forgive today?

Dear Jesus,

Show me what true love is. Help me love those who have hurt me as You have loved me. Forgive me for the way I've hurt others in the past, and stop me from making mistakes in the present. Wipe the slate clean and show me how to forgive as You forgive. Amen.

Read Matthew 5:43-48. Who needs your forgiveness today? How would letting go of the past change *you*?

_____

_____

_____

_____

_____

_____

_____

_____

_____

_____

"How come a woman's default coping mechanism after a breakup or rejection is to declare him a jerk? Is it something they're saying for the sake of self-preservation, or is it actually something they believe?"—*Stefan, 21*

THE REBOUND

An open rebuke is better than hidden love!
Wounds from a sincere friend are better
than many kisses from an enemy.

PROVERBS 27:5-6

Nothing helps soothe the wounds of a broken relationship better than a new one. Instead of dealing with all the tangled emotions that accompany a broken heart, it's just easier to put them aside and move on!

But moving on to a new relationship before dealing with the lessons of the first leaves everyone more broken than they need to be. How can you offer your whole self to a person if your heart still belongs to someone else? How can you fully embrace and rejoice in a new relationship if you're still licking your wounds? It's not fair to you or to the new person in your life.

The kind of distraction a rebound offers—and the wounds and bitterness it covers up—puts you on a detour from your pursuit of a godly relationship. Jesus, after all, wants to bless you with something more than temporary distraction! Check out Matthew 6:33: "Seek the Kingdom of God above all else, and live righteously, and he will give you everything you need." *Everything*. Every desire, fulfilled. Every hope, realized. Every longing, satisfied.

In a rebound, you're not coming to the relationship offering your whole self. It's a sad imitation of the joy that Christ wants to fill us with. In the same way, God calls us to bring our whole selves to Him. In the Gospel of Luke we're reminded that "You must love the LORD your God with all your heart, all your soul, all your strength, and all your mind" (Luke 10:27). Are you ready to bring your whole, complete self into your relationship with God? He won't accept any pretension or half-hearted offerings. Your Savior wants all of you. Will you give yourself to Him today?

Dear Jesus,

No matter what wounds I carry from the past, help me to replace the pain with a deeper relationship with You. Bring people around me to do life together—quick! Don't let me sulk in loneliness or isolate myself because of past hurts. Amen.

Read 2 Peter 1:5-8. Which one of God's promises will you keep hold of today? How can you respond to that promise?

_____

_____

_____

_____

_____

_____

_____

_____

_____

_____

"Why don't you wait until you are ready to date seriously instead of dating randomly?"—*Sharon, 22*

IT'S COMPLICATED!

Both of Lot's daughters became
pregnant by their own father.

GENESIS 19:36

The Bible is full of complicated relationships. Check out the story of Lot and his daughters in Genesis 19, right after the destruction of Sodom and Gomorrah. The daughters were worried that they'd never be able to marry and have children, so they got their father drunk and slept with him. I first heard about Lot in Sunday school, but my teacher only told us the first half of the story. I guess that flannel board couldn't explain the concept of *It's complicated!*

Or take the story of David and Bathsheba in 2 Samuel 11. King David is wandering around his rooftop and sees "a woman of unusual beauty"—Bathsheba—bathing. The king sends for her, sleeps with her, and gets her pregnant. And then, to cover up his sin, he arranges for her husband to be killed in battle. Talk about complicated!

But look what God does with that complicated relationship. Look how he transforms two broken people. David and Bathsheba had a son together—Solomon, the wisest man who ever lived. And that son was the ancestor of the Messiah (Matthew 1:6).

I've met a lot of wonderful couples who have strong marriages, and I've met single people who are perfectly content. But they didn't always start out that way. There were a lot of complications along the way, and a lot of struggles with God's will. Every healthy relationship has a strong foundation, and building that foundation takes a lot of time and a lot of work. But no matter how many bumps and obstacles and *It's complicateds* you encounter along the way, the Creator of the universe will be able to incorporate your mistakes into His great plan.

Dear Jesus,

You stay the same, yesterday, today, and forever. Thank You that Your love covers all mistakes, complications, and failed attempts. Redeem my past relationships. In Your name I pray, Amen.

Read 2 Samuel 11. How have you seen God use your mistakes in His plan for your life?

_____

_____

_____

_____

_____

_____

_____

_____

_____

"I never dreamed God would give me four beautiful children after two abortions and a divorce. My husband and our six children are a daily reminder of His redemption."—*Jennifer, 29*

LISTEN

Get all the advice and instruction you can, so
you will be wise the rest of your life.

PROVERBS 19:20

Have you ever been the third wheel? Sitting across the table from a happy couple? If you're single, it seems that no matter what you do or who you hang around with, you're stuck. Labeled. *The hopeless romantic*.

When I was in my early twenties my best friends Amy, Rachel, and Summer all got married. I never in a million years thought I would be the single friend. I planned to get married young and have kids within a few years. Skip to now. I'm 28 years old. I have a killer career, a ministry, and no husband. It took years for God to mature me and make me ready for my future husband. All those years I'd be hanging out with my "couple" friends, trying to be content as the third wheel, and it took every ounce of strength I had not to run. Then something really cool happened. *I learned*. Observed. Solomon said we should get all the advice and instruction we can, *especially* while we're young. I got a front row seat to the early years of my friends' marriages, watching how they resolved conflict, worked through issues, and began a life together.

Relationships aren't always black and white, and everyone's at a different place in life. Some people choose to court. Some date. Some make mistakes and end up pregnant. No matter where you or I fall on the spectrum, God gives us the gift of one another. "So let's not get tired of doing what is good. At just the right time we will reap a harvest of blessing if we don't give up. Therefore, whenever we have the opportunity, we should do good to everyone—especially to those in the family of faith" (Galatians 6:9-10).

Dear Jesus,

Thank You for filling us with Your Holy Spirit. Remind us that it is necessary to meet together, have fellowship, sing and make music to You. Help us give thanks for everything we do or say in Your name, Jesus. Amen.

Read Hebrews 10:23-25. Who in your life motivates *you* to "acts of love and good works"? How do they live out their example?

_____

_____

_____

_____

_____

_____

_____

_____

"I was the third wheel at a New Year's party. Everyone had someone to kiss at midnight, and I just sat there on the couch feeling like an idiot."—*Abby, 26*

SO YOU THINK
your DATE WAS BAD?

Some friends had set me up on a blind date. I took her mini golfing, and I could tell pretty quickly that it wasn't her idea of a good time. I was so nervous that I stuck the scoring pencil in my mouth and started chewing on it like a teething toddler. By the end of the game, the pencil was stripped clear of its paint and was starting to fall apart, and the girl was looking me like I was an escaped convict. —*Tim, 34*

I was on a date with a girl I'd liked for a while, and for reasons I cannot explain I picked up my steak and started to eat it with my bare hands. —*David, 19*

A guy from church asked me out to coffee. On that date he shared with me that he believed me to be an acceptable mate. After I picked my jaw up off of the table, he proceeded to tell me his thoughts on wifely submission, including the command to "service" his every need whenever he desired. I turned down his ever-so-generous offer of marriage. When the check came he told me my portion of the bill was going to be $4.75. —*Melissa, 35*

A friend hooked me up on a blind date with a guy she knew from church. When we got to the restaurant he started talking about professors and friends in the dorm. I realized too late that my date was still in college...and I graduated fifteen years ago! We didn't have all that much to say to each other. —*Annie, 36*

I was set up on a date with a girl I wasn't remotely attracted to. I was trying to keep it civil, but make sure she knew I wasn't interested in her. In the middle of me saying how I was too busy for a relationship at this time, she asked me what kind of weddings I liked. —*Loren, 29*

My friend and her boyfriend set me up with one of his friends, and we all met at a burger place. My friend started feeding her boyfriend curly fries, and before I knew it they were making out, right there in the booth. My date and I couldn't even look at each other. Instead, he slopped mayo all over his chili burger and started licking off everything that was falling off the burger. I wanted to gag. —*Kesha, 33*

I was set up on a blind date, and I was only told the guy's first name. When he arrived, it turned out to be an ex-boyfriend. Our breakup hadn't been a good one. He stormed off, and I sat there feeling awkward. —*Kelly, 31*

On my way to pick up my date I grabbed the wrong jacket, leaving my wallet and cash at home. I was humiliated. My date very graciously paid for everything, and I made it up to her next time we went out! —*Steve, 24*

unequally yoked

Do not be yoked together with unbelievers. For what
do righteousness and wickedness have in common?
Or what fellowship can light have with darkness?

2 Corinthians 6:14 NIV

You've probably already heard the term *unequally yoked*. This is an image that calls up a team of oxen, one much stronger than the other. How can they plow in a straight line if they're not pulling the weight equally? The Bible is pretty clear here. If you are a follower of Jesus Christ, don't enter into a relationship with someone who doesn't believe. You won't be pulling together.

We are called to spread the Good News of Jesus Christ and make disciples of all nations, but not when it comes to dating. There's always a temptation here to be a "missionary dater." "It's okay that he's not a Christian!" you think. "I'll teach him about Jesus!" I've seen it happen many times. Everyone wants to believe she's the exception to the rule. That he's different. But dating someone who doesn't understand the most essential part of your life is a recipe for disaster. I had a friend who brought his unbelieving girlfriend to church and married her. After a few years she decided the "religion" thing wasn't for her. They divorced.

In the Bible, James makes an even bolder statement. "You adulterers! Don't you realize that friendship with the world makes you an enemy of God? I say it again: If you want to be a friend of the world, you make yourself an enemy of God" (James 4:4). Harsh, but true. When we take advantage of the grace of God, taking relationships into our own hands, we put ourselves at risk. Malachi 2:11-12 says, "A detestable thing has been done in Israel and in Jerusalem. The men of Judah have defiled the LORD'S beloved sanctuary by marrying women who worship idols. May the LORD cut off from the nation of Israel every last man who has done this and yet brings an offering to the LORD of Heaven's Armies." We all know those friends who keep their dating life and religious life completely separate. Saturday night and Sunday morning have nothing to do with each other. But there's still hope, says John. "If we claim we have no sin, we are only fooling ourselves and not living in the truth. But if we confess our sins to him, he is faithful and just to forgive us our sins and to cleanse us from all wickedness" (1 John 1:8-9).

Dear Jesus,
I need Your help to test and approve what Your will is—Your
good and perfect will. Show me which relationships are pleas-
ing to you. Keep me from evil. Amen.

Read 2 Corinthians 6:14. Are you living with both light and darkness in your life? What will you have to leave behind in order to embrace a new life with God?

_____

_____

_____

_____

_____

_____

_____

_____

"I am struggling in an unequally yoked relationship and
I don't know what to do. There are seeds of doubt in
my mind, but I'm trying to reject them."—*Anne, 20*

NOT EVEN A HINT

But among you there must not be
even a hint of sexual immorality.

EPHESIANS 5:3 NIV

I was taught from a very young age that boys and girls shouldn't sleep in the same room. So when a former roommate invited her boyfriend to sleep over on the couch, I was furious. What if I had walked out of my room in my pajamas? (Or without them?) I trusted her to make wise choices, so I tried to understand her perspective. It was getting late and she didn't want him driving home, worrying that he would fall asleep at the wheel and crash. But then it happened again. And again. I was not having it. I thought it was highly inappropriate for a guy to just crash at his girlfriend's apartment. Plus...what would our neighbors think?

How do we set a Christian example? I know some Christians believe it is okay for a dating couple to sleep in the same apartment or even in the same bed. Even if you beat the system and just cuddle, you're setting each other up for future temptation. David, a man after God's own heart, committed adultery with Bathsheba and tried to cover it up by murdering her husband. After that experience of sin and shame he wrote, "How can a young person stay pure? By obeying your word" (Psalm 119:9). And that Word calls us to be holy, for Christ is holy (1 Peter 1:15-16).

"Stay away from all sexual sin," we're warned. "Then each of you will control his own body and live in holiness and honor—not in lustful passion like the pagans who do not know God and his ways" (1 Thessalonians 4:3-5). We are to avoid the appearance of *every* evil. We're called to "live in such a way that no one will stumble because of us, and no one will find fault with our ministry" (2 Corinthians 6:3).

Dear Jesus,

Don't let me play with fire. Show me how to set up appropriate boundaries, and please keep me accountable! Don't let me hide my sin from others. Let me come straight to You and confess my sins. I want to become whole again. Amen.

Read 2 Corinthians 6:3. What are the areas in your life that could cause another person to stumble? Would the world know you were a Christian solely by your actions?

_____

_____

_____

_____

_____

_____

_____

_____

_____

"Keeping things in the dark will only make your issues more difficult to deal with. Don't isolate yourself."—*Matthew, 25*

pure

Put to death the sinful, earthly things lurking
within you. Have nothing to do with sexual
immorality, impurity, lust, and evil desires.

COLOSSIANS 3:5

Look at any magazine or commercial, and you'll see that what's really advertised is *sex*. I'm not the first person to point out that our media is obsessed with it. You'd have to live under a rock to escape all the images that bombard our minds. (Actually, that's where I grew up...but that's beside the point.)

God, of course, calls us to a different lifestyle. Paul instructs us to "Run from sexual sin! No other sin so clearly affects the body as this one does. For sexual immorality is a sin against your own body. Don't you realize that your body is the temple of the Holy Spirit, who lives in you and was given to you by God?" (1 Corinthians 6:18-19). The church is counter-cultural, preaching a message that the secular world can't understand.

But that message isn't always welcomed. How many people had purity rings in high school? How many people took an abstinence pledge?...And how many people put those purity rings away once they got to college?

I believe abstinence is a noble commitment to make as a teenager, but much harder to live out as a young adult. We have more opportunities for independence, and if we don't know where our confidence lies and secure our strong foundation in Christ, we won't fully understand why God asks us to honor Him with our body. God is stronger than our physical passions, and if He's calling you to celibacy at this time in your life, be encouraged! The countercultural church of Jesus Christ is standing behind you, cheering you on.

Dear Jesus,

You care about my body. You're not some vindictive God up in heaven, giving me an impossible command or ultimatum. No matter how difficult it is to treat my body as a temple of the Holy Spirit, it is possible because You said so. Help me believe it! Amen.

Read 1 Corinthians 6:12-20. How can you honor God with your body?

_____

_____

_____

_____

_____

_____

_____

_____

_____

"Happiness is a feeling that comes and goes; contentedness is a choice. It's easy to think I'd be 'happier' if I were in a relationship, but I've decided to be content in the knowledge that God knows the perfect time and who the perfect guy will be."—*Chelsea, 20*

CONFRONT THE LIES

"But I say, anyone who even looks at a woman with lust
has already committed adultery with her in his heart."

MATTHEW 5:28

When Jesus gave the famous Sermon on the Mount, He did not speak flattering words or perform miracles. Nope. He told people to gouge out their eyes and cut off their hands. He radically challenged the cultural mindset and he's still challenging ours. Christ is interested in the condition of our hearts. An evil thought, he says, is no better than an evil deed. Temptation and the lure of sin will entice your mind into action, but "when you are tempted, [God] will show you a way out so that you can endure" (1 Corinthians 10:13).

How's your thought life? Are you facing temptation today? What lies have you believed? Maybe "I can have sex without being emotionally involved," or "Sex will make me feel better." "I'm only hurting myself," you say, or "I need this to feel valued."

Jesus confronts those secrets and lies head-on. He calls them into the light and names them for what they are. Here's the truth: Every person you sleep with is a person you'll be bringing into your marriage bed.

God created marriage to be a sacred union between two people. Taking sex out of that context diminishes and degrades it. Keep that marriage bed pure, and your future spouse will thank you for it. Better yet—keep your *heart* pure. God knows all the secrets it's holding, and is calling you to something better. Something more lovely. Something that will satisfy in a way that cheap sex and one-night stands never could. So when you're tempted, take that way out!

Dear Jesus,

Thank You for pleading with me to give my body to You. Thank You for keeping me from copying the behaviors and customs of this world. Give me the courage to allow You to transform the way I think so I can understand Your good, pleasing, and perfect will. Amen.

Read Matthew 5:27-30. What secrets and lies are you holding close that are causing you to stumble? What would it take for you to reject those lies?

_____

_____

_____

_____

_____

_____

_____

"Having a one-night stand made me feel I was a waste of space. I felt useless and unwanted, and there was a void inside that couldn't be filled no matter how many guys I slept with."—*Katie, 28*

THE BROKEN PLACE

"I live in the high and holy place with those
whose spirits are contrite and humble. I restore
the crushed spirit of the humble and revive the
courage of those with repentant hearts."

ISAIAH 57:15

When we repent and draw near to God, He restores us. We're forgiven. Brand new. Though our sins were like scarlet, we have been made as clean as snow. Whiter than white.

We can get pretty broken before we're willing to come to that place of repentance, though. I've talked to so many young adults who've begun relationships with the best of intentions. They're going to put purity first. But somewhere along the line communication stops and the physical sparks fly. "I have needs" becomes their mantra.

I've seen the pain written all over their face as the relationship turns sour. I've seen the hurt as others—mainly those within the church—judge them. If you've dealt with that kind of brokenness, look to Christ. Jesus never treated someone in need with disgust or disdain. He welcomed beggars and prostitutes with open arms and told them to "go and sin no more" (John 8:11). He was not wishy-washy about the person's sin or the state of their heart, but neither did He point the finger. No matter where you are, Jesus is waiting for *you*. The Bible says, "The Lord isn't really being slow about his promise, as some people think. No, he is being patient for your sake. He does not want anyone to be destroyed, but wants everyone to repent" (2 Peter 3:9).

Next time you're feeling the itch to pull your old life closer, remember Jesus's example. Remember His forgiveness. Remember the fulfillment that only He can provide.

Dear Jesus,

Thank You for forgiving me and making all things new. I choose to follow You and Your ways today. I want to find rest for my mind, body, and soul. Help me to be careful of how I treat others. Amen.

Read 2 Corinthians 7:10-11. What godly sorrow have you experienced in your life? How has it compelled you to make changes?

_____

_____

_____

_____

_____

_____

_____

_____

"Why do girls assume that guys will think and act the same way they do? It's hard to have someone angry at me, especially when she won't even tell me why!"—*Nathan, 29*

perfect Love

Then the Lord God made a woman from the
rib, and he brought her to the man. "At last!" the
man exclaimed. "This one is bone from my
bone, and flesh from my flesh! She will be called
'woman,' because she was taken from 'man.'"

GENESIS 2:22-23

The story of God's love for His people—a love so great that He sent His Son to die for us—is the greatest love story ever told. Check out Romans 5:8: "But God showed his great love for us by sending Christ to die for us while we were still sinners." *While we were still sinners*. Guilty of every kind of evil, our souls black and tarnished...and God sent His perfect, blameless Son for us.

But Jesus did more than just save us from our sin. He exposed our hearts—all the secret shame we keep hidden—and taught us how to love. No matter what kind of relationship we're dealing with—friend, parent, teacher, coworker, lover—we find that relationship's perfect example in Christ Jesus. The love that He exemplified for us "has no fear, because perfect love expels all fear. If we are afraid, it is for fear of punishment, and this shows that we have not fully experienced his perfect love. We love each other because he loved us first" (1 John 4:18-19). Did you catch that? We believe *in* love because Christ loved us—perfectly—first.

When a husband and wife imitate that perfect love that Jesus showed us, we say they're *soul mates*. A couple grows into that kind of relationship by living, learning, working, laughing, and crying together. Jesus calls you into the same relationship. He calls you to grow with Him, and to let Him fill you with His perfect love.

Dear Jesus,

*Show me the worth and weight of true love found only in You,
and when I am tempted to believe otherwise, remind me of
what You did on the cross to pay the penalty for my sins. Amen.*

Read 1 John 4:7-18. Who is the person you love most in this world?
How does your relationship reflect Christ's love for you?

_____

_____

_____

_____

_____

_____

_____

_____

_____

"My girlfriend and I have been dating for over a year now
and I really think she may be 'the one.'"—*Steven, 20*

SOUL TIE

Dear children, keep away from anything that
might take God's place in your hearts.

1 JOHN 5:21

When God created Adam and Eve, He created them to be united together. The Bible says that when "a man leaves his father and mother and is united to his wife...they become one flesh" (Genesis 2:24 NIV). *One flesh*. When two people sleep together their souls and their bodies are tied up into each other. This "mystery of one flesh" is one of the greatest gifts God gave us, and it's worth saving for marriage. When used outside of God's plan, hearts and bodies can become broken almost beyond repair.

I can't tell you how many phone calls I've received from friends who went outside God's plan for marriage. I've listened to them sobbing on the other end of the line and wished I had a way to soothe their suffering. God says in His Word that He always gives us a way out, but we have a choice to take that escape route—or not. You can choose today to walk in the freedom Jesus already bought and paid for.

While you wait for the man or woman of your dreams to come into your life, you can participate in another mystery. When Paul talks about husbands and wives in Ephesians, he says that the union of two people in marriage "is a profound mystery—but I am talking about Christ and the church" (Ephesians 5:32). You can have all of Christ you want, and you can have Him today. Embrace Christ and His community—the fellowship of believers all over the world.

84

Dear Jesus,

Don't let me give the enemy any ground. Renew my mind through Your Word. Teach me how to take my thoughts captive—no matter how fast the lies and thoughts of the enemy come. Renew my relationships today in Your name. Amen.

Read Psalm 51. Where do you need Christ's restoration in your life?

_____

_____

_____

_____

_____

_____

_____

_____

"I was once in a relationship that turned out not to be as healthy as I thought. It wrecked my health and my emotions, and sent me in a tailspin of despair. Only by the grace of God was I able to recover and be set free."—*Amy Marie, 28*

THE LIST

Faith is the confidence that what we
hope for will actually happen; it gives us
assurance about things we cannot see.

HEBREWS 11:1

When I was a kid I made a list of all the qualities I was looking for in a mate. I didn't get much further than *tall, dark hair, light eyes.* When I got older, I added other words to the list. *Leader. Communicator. Compassionate. Encouraging.* I kept building it out, describing my perfect man. *Wants children. Virgin. Well-read. Likes to cook. Doesn't smoke. Doesn't swear. Comes from a Christian family. Good hygiene. Pays his bills on time. Has a heart for ministry.*

None of those qualities are bad, of course, but over time I started to understand that by holding every man to my impossibly high standard, I was putting God into a box. I was turning my back on all the ways He could surprise me and saying, "This way, God, and no other."

Life never turns out the way we expect. Back in school my best friends, Jenn and Amy, and I predicted that I would get married first, followed by Jenn, then Amy. Well, Amy got married first, Jenn became a single mom, and I remained single. God wants to give us the desires of our hearts, but the fulfillment of those desires doesn't always happen at the precise time or in the exact way we expected.

A list has its good points. It will help you define what you want and what you need to avoid. It will help you stay focused and keep you from being distracted, or maybe compromising on someone who won't lead you closer to God. But don't be so tied to your own plans and sense of timing that you forget to trust in God's.

Dear Jesus,

I need to trust in You to provide and not place unrealistic expectations on those around me. Give me an extra measure of discernment today, I pray. Amen.

Read Philippians 4:8. What's on your list? Write down some characteristics, traits, and qualities you're looking for (or have found) in a mate.

_____

_____

_____

_____

_____

_____

_____

_____

"Why are women so impatient to find
the right guy?"—*Rob, 28*

Fairy Tale

And I am certain that God, who began the good work
within you, will continue his work until it is finally
finished on the day when Christ Jesus returns.

PHILIPPIANS 1:6

Life is never easy for characters in fairy tales. The prince has to rescue a princess from a tower, or do battle with a fiery dragon. The princess has to outwit a wicked witch or find a way to break the enchantment. The maidservant has to find a way to get the prince to notice her, and the stable boy has to outwit the cruel stepmother. And there might be a few ogres along the way.

Walt Disney once said that Cinderella "believed in dreams, all right, but she also believed in doing something about them. When Prince Charming didn't come along, she went over to the palace and got him." Part of growing up is taking the first step on that epic journey, not knowing where it will take us. There's more to the story than the kiss at the end, after all.

When we put as much effort into discovering the heart of God as we do to examining our love lives, we become the best version of ourselves. The more time I spend plotting how to attract the attention of the latest Prince Charming in my life, the more I miss out on the rich, powerful, unending love of God.

In Proverbs 4:25-27, Solomon tells us to "Look straight ahead, and fix your eyes on what lies before you. Mark out a straight path for your feet; stay on the safe path. Don't get sidetracked; keep your feet from following evil." Where is the journey leading you today? Ask God to take your hand and walk beside you, no matter how much fire the dragon breathes or how deep the enchantment may be.

Dear Jesus,

I crave an adventure with You. Help me stay on the narrow path. No matter how difficult it is, don't let me stray to the left or to the right. Keep my feet from evil! Amen.

Read Philippians 1:6. What's the story Christ is telling through your life? What kind of happy ending do you envision?

_____

_____

_____

_____

_____

_____

_____

_____

"I'm afraid that I will never find the guy God has for me—or that the guy He has for me will not be who I'd like it to be. I gave my heart away instead of guarding it like I should have."—*Dawn, 28*

A GOD-SIZED ADVENTURE

For the LORD has called you back from
your grief—as though you were a young
wife abandoned by her husband.

ISAIAH 54:6

Sleeping Beauty lies in bed sleeping while Prince Charming fights his way past fearsome beasts and briars to rescue her. Rapunzel combs her hair in the tower while she waits for her prince to kill the wicked witch. Snow White lies in a *coffin*, dead to the world, until her prince shows up to kiss her awake. The list goes on and on, until we actually start to believe it. I sure believed I would marry a prince and live happily ever after. But as these fairy tales turned out to be just stories, I had to look around to see what else was out there.

And for me, what was out there was more lies. More pain. I was missing huge chunks of skin, my body wasn't cooperating, and I gained 100 pounds in ten months. Lies were all I heard. "You're never going to find somebody to love you." "God has left you. He's abandoned you. He doesn't care about you." I looked in the mirror and believed those lies. On and on they went until I laid down my hurt and surrendered my pride. I learned once again how to find comfort in the arms of my God. And I realized I wasn't really living the kind of adventure God had for me. Check out what the prophet Isaiah says about this adventure: "Fear not; you will no longer live in shame. Don't be afraid; there is no more disgrace for you. You will no longer remember the shame of your youth... For your Creator will be your husband; the LORD of Heaven's Armies is his name! He is your Redeemer, the Holy One of Israel, the God of all the earth" (Isaiah 54:4-5).

This kind of God will give you an epic adventure—a God-sized adventure—and will take you places you never dreamed. Throw off the lies today. A flesh-and-blood prince isn't coming to rescue you from a tower, but the God of the Universe is coming to take your hand and your heart. Life will never be boring with Him. So what do you say? Will you live your God-sized adventure?

Dear Jesus,

The epic tale of love awaits. You are my Royal Husband and I am Yours and Yours alone. I long for the day when I will spend eternity with You. Keep me pure and steadfast until then, and keep me living the God-sized adventure. Amen.

Read Isaiah 54:4-10. Are you living a God-sized adventure? Why or why not?

_____

_____

_____

_____

_____

_____

_____

_____

_____

"How do guys know a girl is worth it—whether getting up the courage to ask her out, or to be their girlfriend, or propose?"—*Danielle, 22*

secure

Don't copy the behavior and customs of this world, but
let God transform you into a new person by changing
the way you think. Then you will learn to know God's
will for you, which is good and pleasing and perfect.

ROMANS 12:2

I know I'm not the only person around who suffers from something
I like to call IDD—Insecurity Dysfunctional Disorder. People can be
insecure about their looks, their relationship status, their family, their
résumé, their singing voice…anything. Everything.

It hit me recently that my insecurity only breeds more fear. I need
to replace my IDD mentality with different words. *I'm worth sacrificing
for. I'm worth loving. I'm worth the wait. I am worthy.* I tried out my
new mantra on a casual date. Instead of being my normal insecure self,
I acted confident—more confident than I felt! My coffee date took one
look at me and told me how pretty I was. *Wow.* And that was within the
first five seconds. Imagine what I could do with five minutes!

Isn't it amazing how God gives you a gift—even a seemingly little
one—at just the right time? I want to give you a few verses to hold on
to next time you feel insecure. Write the verses down on 3x5 cards and
place them somewhere you'll see them regularly—on your bathroom
mirror, bulletin board, or the dashboard of your car.

- "There is no condemnation for those who belong to
  Christ Jesus" (Romans 8:1).

- "It is God who enables us…to stand firm for Christ"
  (2 Corinthians 1:21-22).

- "God, who began the good work within you, will continue
  his work until it is finally finished" (Philippians 1:6).

- "We are citizens of heaven" (Philippians 3:20).
- "For God has not given us a spirit of fear and timidity, but of power, love, and self-discipline" (2 Timothy 1:7).
- "So let us come boldly to the throne of our gracious God. There we will receive his mercy, and we will find grace to help us when we need it most" (Hebrews 4:16).

The more you reaffirm who you are in Christ, the more your behavior will begin to reflect your true identity. Rest today in the security and ultimate assurance of God's love for you.

Dear Jesus,

Before I start my day, bring the verses to mind that I need to stand and make it through victoriously. Help me live in the light and make my joy complete as I come into fellowship with You and other believers today. Amen.

Read Romans 12:1-3. What are your secret insecurities? What would your life look like if you could give all those fears to God?

_____

_____

_____

_____

_____

_____

_____

"I didn't understand how someone could like
me just for me and not for what I could do
or what I could offer them."—*Ronel, 31*

GIVe anD TaKe

Take delight in the LORD, and he will
give you your heart's desires.

PSALM 37:4

I was reading the book *Big God,* by Britt Merrick, and came across this line: "God is a giver, not a taker. For everything that I surrendered to Him, He blessed me with far more than I could have ever imagined."* If that's how gracious and giving God is, shouldn't I be following His example? I'm proud by nature. I take. I love to receive. God says He'll give me the desires of my heart, but I'd like to follow my own direction, thank you very much.

A person who gives doesn't act like other people. He or she is imitating God instead of the world. Just watch how they treat other people. Is she kind to her parents? Does he respect authority? Does she discriminate, or does she choose to serve? The giving personality understands that it's more blessed to give than receive. They choose not to be served. What about you?

In my pride, I never thought in a million years that God could give me the desires of my heart. I didn't believe that God would be able to get around my plans and defenses and surprise me with joy, but He has... and it's the best feeling in the world. I am giving to others in ministry and being blessed in return. God knows the best way for me to bring glory to Him, and who am I to get upset at the Potter when I am the clay?

---

*Britt Merrick, *Big God* (Ventura, CA: Regal, 2010), 99.

Dear Jesus,

You are the great Giver, lavishing every good thing upon me. Help me to be as generous and giving today as You are. Surprise me with Your grace today, Lord. Amen.

Read Matthew 5:43-48. Is there someone in your life you have difficulty loving? What can you do today to become more giving in your relationship?

_____

_____

_____

_____

_____

_____

_____

_____

_____

"I never thought God could bring me this kind of happiness. But He brought someone into my life who is so amazing, so perfect for just me! Every day, I am surprised by His blessings."—*Stephanie, 29*

questions, questions

Don't use foul or abusive language. Let everything
you say be good and helpful, so that your words will
be an encouragement to those who hear them.

EPHESIANS 4:29

This whole dating thing can be overwhelming. Out of all the men or women in the world, how are you supposed to pick the one perfect person? How can you ever know for sure? Here are a few questions to ask about a potential date or significant other.

Does he or she have a teachable spirit? "My child, don't reject the LORD's discipline, and don't be upset when he corrects you" (Proverbs 3:11).

Does he or she live under God's authority? "Everyone must submit to governing authorities. For all authority comes from God, and those in positions of authority have been placed there by God. So anyone who rebels against authority is rebelling against what God has instituted, and they will be punished" (Romans 13:1-2).

Does he or she have a clear conscience? "Young people, it's wonderful to be young! Enjoy every minute of it. Do everything you want to do; take it all in. But remember that you must give an account to God for everything you do" (Ecclesiastes 11:9).

Is he or she good with children? "Anyone who welcomes a little child like this on my behalf is welcoming me" (Matthew 18:5).

Is he or she financially free? "Give to everyone what you owe them: Pay your taxes and government fees to those who collect them, and give respect and honor to those who are in authority" (Romans 13:7).

Is he or she able to pray with and for you? "Confess your sins to each other and pray for each other so that you may be healed. The earnest prayer of a righteous person has great power and produces wonderful results" (James 5:16).

Ask these questions often, and don't be afraid to have deep conversations. Relationships that establish communication as a value and priority are more likely to succeed when trouble comes.

Dear Jesus,

Give me discernment in all things—especially when choosing a life partner! Help me to look at each person's heart, acknowledging their weaknesses and celebrating their triumphs. Help me to look at others the way You see them. Amen.

Read Ephesians 4:17-32. How have you seen God working to shape you into the kind of person someone would desire to spend his or her life with?

_____

_____

_____

_____

_____

_____

_____

"Why can't women just say exactly what they're thinking or feeling? Why does everything have to be in code?"—Adam, 21

BUILT ON THE ROCK

If you think you are standing
strong, be careful not to fall.

1 CORINTHIANS 10:12

We all need spiritual leaders and authorities in our lives. People to build you up, show you the way, and keep you from falling too far. In a dating relationship—as well as a marriage—Christ needs to be the head.

When couples date, questions will always arise. Tough questions, like: "How far is too far? Where do I draw the line with physical purity?" "Who is going to keep me accountable to the boundaries I set for myself? For the boundaries we set as a couple?" "What if he or she is the one and we're going to get married eventually? Does it even matter if we sleep together before the wedding?"

Your purity, as an individual and as a couple, matters, and outside of Christ who could hope to hold on to their convictions? A little temptation goes a long way. Solomon asked, "Can a man scoop a flame into his lap and not have his clothes catch on fire?" (Proverbs 6:27). With Christ at the head of your relationship, you'll both be able to look forward at Him instead of only at each other. Christ will keep you from scooping that flame into your lap in the first place.

A relationship built on Christ is able to weather any storm, to stand and keep on standing (Epheians 6:13). When the problems of life come along—conflict, miscommunication, unmet or unrealistic expectations, or any kind of family problems—a couple whose foundation is in Christ will make it through. Get in the habit of praying together as a couple. Set up boundaries together so *when* you're faced with temptation you'll have a way out.

Dear Jesus,

You are my leader. Let everything I do and say be a reflection of my relationship with You. Teach me how to be wise and not to act thoughtlessly in my relationships. Amen.

Read Ephesians 5:15-21. What would your day look like if it was spent in total devotion to God and His will? How can you keep Him at the center today?

_____

_____

_____

_____

_____

_____

_____

_____

_____

> "I've been in a relationship for about two years with a wonderful Christian man who points me to Jesus."—*Emily, 21*

THE BAD BOY

Don't worry about the wicked or envy those who do wrong. For like grass, they soon fade away. Like spring flowers, they soon wither.

PSALM 37:1-2

You know what I mean by "The Bad Boy." He's handsome. He's confident. And he can so easily lead a woman astray.

I've heard a number of guys—good, decent, clean-cut guys that any woman would be happy to call her boyfriend—wonder why women are always attracted to "bad boys"—guys who only seem destined to hurt them. Let's take a closer look at this dynamic.

The bad boy possesses charm. He knows how to make a girl feel attractive and adored. He knows exactly what to say and how to say it.

The bad boy leads. Women respond to a guy who pursues. As little girls we're taught to let the guy initiate.

The bad boy breaks all the rules. There's an element of danger in his personality that keeps women on edge, waiting to see what happens next.

The bad boy is a challenge. For all those ladies who aren't happy in their career or current relationship, or who are just looking for an escape, the bad boy looks pretty good. The woman wants to reform him, but only hurts herself in the process.

Most women have a 68,245-point checklist for what they want in a man. But if they meet the right guy, they might throw it all away in hopes of "changing" their bad boy. It doesn't work.

Protect your heart, ladies. Don't give it away to someone who won't hold it carefully. And guys, work to be deserving of that heart. You don't have to hurt a girl to hold her.

Dear Jesus,

Help me to remember my worth, and help me to look to You alone for adventure, excitement, and fulfillment. Amen.

Read Titus 2:6-8. How can you be an example of godly living today?

_____

_____

_____

_____

_____

_____

_____

_____

"Good girls always fall for the bad boys because it's exciting, fun, and there is never a dull moment. But that doesn't mean it's a good thing."—*Marie, 28*

Mr. Nice Guy

"Don't judge by his appearance or height, for I
have rejected him. The LORD doesn't see things
the way you see them. People judge by outward
appearance, but the LORD looks at the heart."

1 SAMUEL 16:7

It's a common rule that "nice guys finish last." They don't have that edge, that sexy devil-may-care attitude that gives the bad boys their appeal. But if nice guys finish last in our culture...well, check out what the Bible says happens to the bad boys. "Though the wicked sprout like weeds and evildoers flourish, they will be destroyed forever" (Psalm 92:7). Yup. Bad boys don't finish *at all*.

The nice guy might feel like he's getting left behind, but his integrity, morality, and strong principles will steer him through. "Follow the steps of good men instead, and stay on the paths of the righteous. For only the godly will live in the land, and those with integrity will remain in it," says Solomon (Proverbs 2:20-21).

The nice guy—the *godly* guy—respects his girlfriend. He's humble and teachable, and always striving to better himself for God and for the woman he loves. He's upright and lives beyond reproach. He keeps Christ at the center of the relationship, knowing that "in him all things hold together" (Colossians 1:17 NIV). He seeks godly advice from wise teachers. He is cautious and self-controlled, is patient, faithful, and loyal.

If women overlook him to go after the wild ride instead, they'll find that the adventure is short-lived. The Bible says, "It is better to be godly and have little than to be evil and rich. For the strength of the wicked will be shattered, but the LORD takes care of the godly" (Psalm 37:16-17). If you're a nice guy who's been single for a while, be encouraged. The maturity process takes time, but your character will shine through in the end.

Dear Jesus,

It's hard not to take the wrong path. Everywhere I look it seems that people are desperate for pleasure. Keep me moving forward in wisdom while focusing my eyes straight ahead. Amen.

Read Proverbs 2:16-22. Where is "the path of the righteous" leading you today?

_____

_____

_____

_____

_____

_____

_____

_____

"Nice guys finish last when their hope is in
the girl and not in Jesus." —*Aaron, 30*

crossroads

Stop at the crossroads and look around. Ask
for the old, godly way, and walk in it. Travel its
path, and you will find rest for your souls.

JEREMIAH 6:16

In Jeremiah 6, the prophet says that Israel is at a crossroads. Have you ever been there? In your professional life, your education, your dating relationships? Has there been a time when you faced a number of options, all of which looked equally attractive but presented wildly different futures? Maybe one path looked easy—a college close to home, a job in the same building where you'd been an intern, dating the pastor's daughter. Maybe the other path was more uncertain—a college in a different part of the country, a career that wasn't certain to bring financial stability, dating a guy your parents couldn't stand.

Jeremiah has advice for Israel and for you. Check out his instructions in verse 16:

Stop. Recognize the crossroads right in front of you. Before you make a decision, take some time to reflect and seek God's will.

Look. Immediate distractions or hindrances directly in front of us might cause us to miss the right path.

Ask. Talk to God and people you trust. Seek wise counsel. Dig into the Word. This part's important. Hebrews 2:1 warns us that "we must listen very carefully to the truth we have heard, or we may drift away from it."

Walk. Once you're certain of God's will, take those first steps on the path with confidence.

Travel. Once you've made all the preparations, you can enjoy the journey and delight in all the surprise and abundance you find along the way.

When you reach a crossroads in your life, find peace and certainty by following God's will!

> *Dear Jesus,*
>
> *There are so many decisions and possibilities in front of me today. I cannot trust my emotions. Give me the wisdom I need to help me choose the right path, and walk with me no matter which way I go. Amen.*

Read Jeremiah 6:16-19. What crossroads are you facing in your life? How can you discern the godly path?

_____

_____

_____

_____

_____

_____

_____

_____

"Do guys even desire to do the traditional dating anymore? Why don't they ask women out on dates instead of going out in groups or just casually hanging out?"—*Sarah, 31*

Drama Queen

In the end she is as bitter as poison.

PROVERBS 5:4

*D*rama. We've all got it in our lives. Who said what, who made out with whom, who broke up with whom…we can't get away from it. But we're certainly warned not to indulge in it. Check out how Solomon describes the "immoral woman." (I like to call her "The Drama Queen.")

> For the lips of an immoral woman are as sweet as honey,
> and her mouth is smoother than oil. But in the end she
> is as bitter as poison,
> as dangerous as a double-edged sword.
> Her feet go down to death;
> her steps lead straight to the grave.
> For she cares nothing about the path to life.
> She staggers down a crooked trail and doesn't realize it.
> (Proverbs 5:3-6)

Sound like anyone you know? A drama queen loves to draw you into her intrigue. "Let me tell you what happened," she says. She makes you feel like you're on the inside. Her words are "sweet as honey"—but maybe that's because she loves the sound of her own voice.

The drama queen is reckless. She loves to argue just for the sake of arguing, twisting situations and creating misunderstandings between close friends. She thrives on conflict. She'll criticize others to your face, and then turn around and start talking about *you*. She is, in the end, "bitter as poison."

Wherever she is, wherever she goes, trouble follows, right along with grief and heartache. In verse 8, Solomon warns us to "Stay away from her! Don't go near the door of her house!" Instead, pursue godly friendships that are founded in trust, not deception. "Obscene stories, foolish talk, and coarse jokes—these are not for you," says Paul in Ephesians 5:4. "Instead, let there be thankfulness to God." Christ teaches us how to thrive on real human relationships, not drama!

Dear Jesus,

Help me to remember Your words to remain strong, firm, and steadfast in You. Teach me to pursue healthy relationships that are grounded in Your Word. Amen.

Read Proverbs 26:21. Have you ever gotten too involved in someone else's drama? How can you avoid it in the future?

_____

_____

_____

_____

_____

_____

_____

_____

"Why do women have to fill everything with drama?"—*Chuck, 24*

SO YOU THINK *your* DATE WAS BAD?

In the middle of dinner my date got up, said he was going to the bathroom, and left the table. He was gone for half an hour. I started to wonder if he'd ditched me, but his jacket was still on the chair and his phone was still in the pocket. He finally returned with some excuse about feeding the parking meter, acting like nothing was wrong. When the check finally came, he whipped out a two-for-one coupon. "I bet you're glad I have this," he said. "Otherwise I wouldn't have taken you to a place this nice."—*Andrea, 23*

I went to the restroom during dinner, and when I came out the back of my skirt was tucked into my nylons! —*Michelle, 30*

I was on a date with a guy I met on eHarmony. It was really uncomfortable—we had nothing in common, and I had more chemistry with our waiter. As the date was ending he looked at me and said, "So how should we pursue this?" I told him I wasn't interested. —*Chelsea, 26*

I spent the entire date calling a guy by his twin brother's name. Worst date ever for him *and* me. —*Bethany, 32*

I was out with a woman I'd been interested in for a long time, and I wanted to look cool. But when I tried to pay for our dinner my card was declined. I couldn't figure out what was wrong, because I knew I had money in my account. I called the bank, and they asked me to look at my card. It didn't have my name on it! I'd been given the wrong card when I was shopping earlier that day. —*Chuck, 24*

I was in high school and no one had asked me to the homecoming dance. My grandma talked to a friend who had a son my age and got him to ask me out. At the dance, he told all my friends that my grandma set us up. It was awful. —*Shauna, 27*

I was set up and went to pick up my date at her apartment on a Friday night. Somehow I mixed up the dates, because she wasn't expecting me until Saturday. She was sick with a fever, and had crashed on her couch wearing an old bathrobe and surrounded by tissues. I felt awful. —*Jamie, 32*

One night, against my better judgment, I agreed to go out with a guy I met online. He seemed nice enough, opening the door for me and the whole shebang. We got through dinner okay and had a pleasant conversation, but then the check came. He looked at it, turned red, and started flying off the handle about how much it cost. I offered to pay my half, but that didn't help. He called over the waitress and then the manager to ask why it was so high. After making a scene in front of the whole restaurant, screaming at the top of his lungs and cussing out the waitress, he finally decided to pay for half and then leave me there to pay the rest, including the tip. When I looked at the check, it was only $30. I have never wished to be invisible more than I did right then. —*Tabitha, 20*

Greatly Praised

Charm is deceptive, and beauty does not last; but a
woman who fears the LORD will be greatly praised.

PROVERBS 31:30

When I was growing up, I was always the "good girl." I never seriously rebelled against my parents or their authority. I respected them too much to do otherwise.

Scripture has a much more beautiful definition of "the good girl" than "someone who doesn't rebel." She may not stand out right away, but you certainly know one. She could be your BFF, mother, or teacher. Check out what Solomon has to say about the characteristics of a godly woman.

The good girl—Solomon calls her "a wife of noble character"—can be trusted. She enriches her husband's life. She brings good to her family, not harm. She works. She buys land. She is energetic. Strong. Her business is profitable. She stays out of trouble and puts her hands to work. She dresses well and her husband is respected in the city. She's dignified but she knows how to laugh. Her words encourage others, and people go to her for godly advice.

Hello? Who wouldn't want to date this person? Can you think of any women in your life—your mother, grandmother, sister, girlfriend, or significant other—who exemplify a few of these qualities? What is it about her that you admire or find attractive? Take the time to tell her today. Thank her for the work she's done and give her the praise she is due.

Dear Jesus,

You are perfect and Your desire for me, Your child, is to be perfect! Soften my heart to receive Your love, in Jesus's name. Amen.

Read Proverbs 31:10-31. What qualities of this wife of noble character do you most admire? Why? Who in your life exemplifies those qualities?

_____

_____

_____

_____

_____

_____

_____

_____

_____

"With a heart hidden in the Lord, everyone will
know who you belong to."—*Jenny, 21*

ENOUGH

Each time he said, "My grace is all you need. My
power works best in weakness." So now I am
glad to boast about my weaknesses, so that
the power of Christ can work through me.

2 CORINTHIANS 12:9

S usan E. Isaacs, one of my favorite authors, wrote a book called *Angry
Conversations with God: A Snarky but Authentic Spiritual Memoir.*
She doesn't hide anything in her story. Not the pain, not the heartache,
not life's most crushing disappointments. Her brutal honesty mixed
with comedy had me alternately in tears and curled up in spasms of
laughter. Susan didn't pretend to enjoy being single. She hated it. She
even went as far as taking God to couples counseling. Read my favorite part below:

> Susan: I wanted to be loved.
>
> God: So do I, Susan. I have loved you your whole life. I've
> never left you. Even when you wanted me to. I brought you
> out of despair. I dumped so many blessings into your life—
> you had nearly everything. Except one thing: a man. Don't
> you think I knew that? Did you have no patience?*

Ouch. Isn't that what we do? We have everything we need except
_____. How would you fill in that blank? A spouse. A career. Children.
Health. The apostle Paul knew something about this one. He asked God
three times in Scripture to take away his health problems. Paul was desperate. He knew the saving power of God's grace—the power that had
already healed more people than he could count. So why couldn't he be

---

*Susan E. Isaacs, *Angry Conversations With God: A Snarky but Authentic Spiritual Memoir* (New York:
  Hachette, 2009), 162.

healed as well? But instead of lashing out at God, Paul learned to rest in His grace, trusting that he was firmly in the Healer's care.

Is God's grace enough for you? Give Him your pain and anxiety today, trusting in His perfect timing.

> Dear Jesus,
>
> *If Your grace was enough for Paul, shouldn't it be enough for me too? No matter the circumstances, help me to praise You, Lord, for You are gracious and compassionate; slow to anger and filled with unfailing love. Amen.*

Read Habakkuk 3:17-19. What do you feel that your life is lacking? Do you think that God cares about that lack? What blessings can you thank Him for today, even in the midst of your wanting?

_____

_____

_____

_____

_____

_____

_____

_____

"I'd rather die on the mountain than lie around
in Death Valley." *—Susan E. Isaacs*

*Isaacs, *Angry Conversations with God,* 239.

THE RENT

Don't love money; be satisfied with what
you have. For God has said, "I will never
fail you, I will never abandon you."

HEBREWS 13:5

You graduated from college with a degree you loved but wasn't, as your parents warned you, all that much use in the real world. So you got a job that didn't pay much—just a few hundred bucks a week, enough to afford a tiny apartment. Money's tight, but at least you're living on your own!

But along comes this guy. And you really, really want to impress him. So the day before the date, you buy a sexy new dress. You indulge in a mani and pedi. New perfume. New heels to match the new dress.

Or along comes this girl—a girl you really think could be *The One.* You suit up and take her out to the most expensive restaurant in town— the one where you can't read the menu because it's all in French and the waiter turns up his nose when you don't know which wine to order.

…And there goes the rent money!

Where do you spend your money when you're trying to impress someone? God calls us to be responsible with our finances. "Give to everyone what you owe them," says Paul in Romans 13:7. That includes the money for rent, school loans, groceries, and all the other bills that hit your mailbox. If it means you can't afford that mani and pedi, or that you can't cover the tip for the valet, choose a more affordable (and more relaxed) date! Show off your best self, without all the trimmings. If you're responsible with your finances, offering all you can to God, the Lord promises to "pour out a blessing so great you won't have room enough to take it in!" (Malachi 3:10).

Dear Jesus,

Open my eyes to the person I have become. Show me that in the midst of any type of crisis, You are my ultimate Provider— not people. Thank You for showing me that You will never leave or abandon me. Amen.

Read Matthew 6:19-34. What are your needs—not wants—that you trust God will provide for? Do you believe Him when He says He'll give you your daily bread?

_____

_____

_____

_____

_____

_____

_____

_____

_____

"I wish my fiancée and I could go ahead and get married. Stupid financial troubles!"—*Travis, 27*

WHaT HaPPens AFTer 9 PM...

For you are all children of the light and of
the day; we don't belong to darkness and
night. So be on your guard, not asleep like
the others. Stay alert and be clearheaded.

1 Thessalonians 5:5-6

I am not a night person. There is nothing about being up late that I
enjoy. My brain gets foggy, my eyes start drooping, and I just can't
function the next morning. But there's more to an early bedtime than
getting in my beauty sleep. I've found that nothing good happens after
9:00 p.m.

Have you ever been out partying late at night? As the night wears
on, your senses become dulled. You lose your sense of judgment. And
you might do something you'll regret in the light of morning. Solomon warns us, "Do not carouse with drunkards or feast with gluttons,
for they are on their way to poverty" (Proverbs 23:20-21). The kind of
drunken partying that goes on long into the night isn't godly. You're
not doing anything in those situations that you'll be proud of later, or
that will show the people around you that you're following Christ. We're
called to something higher, to give the world a different example of how
to live. "Don't copy the behavior and customs of this world," says Paul,
"but let God transform you into a new person by changing the way you
think. Then you will learn to known God's will for you, which is good
and pleasing and perfect" (Romans 12:2).

If you're the night owl who never stops partying until dawn, God
offers you a different path. God offers you a second chance. When Jesus
lived among us on earth, He hung out with sinners. His friends were tax
collectors—the most despised, dishonest guys around—and prostitutes.
They were people who didn't *deserve* His grace, the religious leaders said.

Jesus "came to seek and save those who are lost" (Luke 19:10), and that includes you and me.

Dear Jesus,

Time is running out. Help me to make the most of my time while I'm here on this earth so when You return I will not shrink back from shame. Amen.

Read Romans 13:11-14. How can you commit yourself to the light today?

_____

_____

_____

_____

_____

_____

_____

_____

"Partying is a great way to meet people and feel good
about yourself in that moment, but in the morning
it feels completely different. Plus, there really are
not too many quality, long-term connections that
come out of the bar scene."—*Tiffany, 21*

wingman

When the watchman sees the enemy coming,
he sounds the alarm to warn the people.

EZEKIEL 33:3

Who's your dearest, closest friend? The one person you could count on in any situation? The man or woman who will always be there when you're in trouble, no matter how inconvenient it is?

That person's responsibility toward you—and yours toward him or her—isn't just to hang out, watch movies together, and have a good time. A friendship that deep requires truth in all things. This is the friend who can warn you away from danger and tell you you're screwing up...and then turn around and buy you that venti latte you've been craving, because she understands how tough life can be.

"A friend is always loyal," says Proverbs 17:17, "and a brother is born to help in time of need." We all need these people in our lives, and we all have friends who need *us* to be the wingman when times are tough. In Ezekiel 33:6 we're warned, "If the watchman sees the enemy coming and doesn't sound the alarm to warn the people...I will hold [him] responsible for their deaths." This isn't a responsibility to take lightly. If you see a friend stumbling (lying, cheating, sleeping around, abusing alcohol or other substances, or engaging in other damaging behaviors) and don't say something because you're afraid of hurting his feelings, you'll be held accountable.

Don't take your watchman/wingman for granted this week. Go out of your way to thank her for the godly presence she is in your life...and maybe buy her that venti latte while you're at it.

Dear Jesus,

I need all the help I can get. Don't let me go through life alone. Bring the right people close to me, and help me to take advantage of their wisdom and courage today. Amen.

Read Ezekiel 33:1-6. What qualities make somebody a good wingman?

_____

_____

_____

_____

_____

_____

_____

_____

_____

"A friend is someone who's there in good times and in bad—when you're trying to complete that big project, move to your new place, or flirt with the cute waiter."—*Heather, 25*

THE GreaT ROManCe

"Kiss me and kiss me again, for your love is
sweeter than wine. How fragrant your cologne;
your name is like its spreading fragrance."

SONG OF SONGS 1:2-3

The Bible is the long, beautiful story of God romancing His people. Let's look today at just one chapter in that story—the story of Moses. You know how it goes: "It was by faith that Moses, when he grew up, refused to be called the son of Pharaoh's daughter. He chose to share the oppression of God's people instead of enjoying the fleeting pleasures of sin. He thought it was better to suffer for the sake of Christ than to own the treasures of Egypt, for he was looking ahead to his great reward" (Hebrews 11:24-26). By the time we catch up to Moses in the wilderness, there are no more palaces, no more rich food, no more servants. He's not a prince anymore; he's just a shepherd. But one day he sees something strange: a bush is on fire, but it's not burning up. Moses can't take his eyes off it. And "When the LORD saw Moses coming to take a closer look, God called to him" (Exodus 3:4).

There are many ways that God romances us, but all that's required of us is to stop and notice the fire. Do you see God? Do you know He is there? Check out what the prophet Zephaniah says: "The LORD your God is living among you. He is a mighty savior. He will take delight in you with gladness. With his love, he will calm all your fears. He will rejoice over you with joyful songs" (Zephaniah 3:17). God romances us by singing over us. He directs our steps, delighting in every detail. In fact, "he will order his angels to protect you wherever you go" (Psalm 91:11). There isn't anything we can do to earn God's love. He is always singing over us, always protecting, always guiding, no matter how far we stray.

Dear Jesus,

You are the divine creator of romance. Show me how to love others the way You love me, Lord. Keep my heart pure and turned toward You. Amen.

Read Psalm 91. How have you felt God romancing you this week?

_____

_____

_____

_____

_____

_____

_____

"A romantic guy is one who seeks lasting joy for his partner—a joy which ends not in herself, but in her enjoying the all-satisfying glory of God." —*Marc, 28*

THe Love Languages

The blessing of the LORD makes a person
rich, and he adds no sorrow with it.

PROVERBS 10:22

When Jesus was asked what the greatest, most important commandment was, he answered, "You must love the LORD your God with all your heart, all your soul, all your mind, and all your strength" (Mark 12:30). These are the *real* love languages. When the apostle John writes about this command, he says, "I am not writing a new commandment for you; rather it is an old one you have heard from the very beginning. This old commandment—to love one another—is the same message you heard before. Yet it is also new. Jesus lived the truth of this commandment, and you also are living it" (1 John 2:7-8).

Ask the Lord to help you love with your *heart*. "I will take away their stony, stubborn heart and give them a tender, responsive heart" (Ezekiel 11:19).

Ask the Lord to help you love with your *soul*. "O God, you are my God; I earnestly search for you. My soul thirsts for you; my whole body longs for you in this parched and weary land where there is no water" (Psalm 63:1).

Ask the Lord to help you love with your *mind*. "Come and listen to my counsel. I'll share my heart with you and make you wise" (Proverbs 1:23).

Ask the Lord to help you love with your *strength*. "Praise the Lord, who is my rock. He trains my hands for war and gives my fingers skill for battle" (Psalm 144:1).

Love is nothing new—not really, even though the first blush of romance certainly *feels* new. God's love is older than the mountains, older than the stars, and yet it's new every morning. When God is your first love, that joy and excitement of romance will never end.

Dear Jesus,

Please search my heart and test my anxious thoughts. Don't let me get away with going too fast too soon. Help me to seek You daily—with all my heart, soul, mind, and strength. Amen.

Read Mark 12:28-34. Where is your heart today?

_____

_____

_____

_____

_____

_____

_____

_____

"I got engaged after a year of dating, and our engagement lasted five months. Even though both of us waited for our wedding night, it felt like five months too long!"—*Amy, 28*

CHOOSING CONTENTMENT

Yet true godliness with contentment
is itself great wealth.

1 TIMOTHY 6:6

Each of you should continue to live in whatever situation the Lord
has placed you, and remain as you were when God first called you"
(1 Corinthians 7:17). Yikes. *A rule?* Maybe we should pay attention.

We're always looking to change our situation. We continually search
online for someone to make us feel loved. We seek that better job, a different career, a cuter apartment. But in all the choices we make, we
should choose to know the Lord. That's the wisest choice of all.

Elyse Fitzpatrick said, "The truth about the choices we make is plain.
We don't consistently choose the Lord because we don't really desire
him...and we don't really desire him because we're not convinced that
choosing him will result in our happiness."* She echoes Paul's words
from Philippians 2:13: "For God is working in you, giving you the desire
and the power to do what pleases him."

Is your desire for a relationship? For a better job? For the latest gad-
get? Or is your desire to work for God's kingdom? When our desires and
our choices are in line with God's plan, we get to serve our Heavenly
Father—*with joy*. This joyful contentment starts with the choices we
make. Daily. If you're in a place in your life where you feel unsatisfied,
use this time to store up treasures in heaven. Don't think for a moment
that contentment is your mother or grandmother's word. Choosing
contentment is tough work, but strive for it anyway. Trust that God can
use you where you are.

---

* Elyse Fitzpatrick, *Idols of the Heart: Learning to Long for God Alone* (Phillipsburg, NJ: P&R Publishing,
2002), 150.

Dear Jesus,

Don't let me believe the lies of the enemy that contentment means giving up! Give me the peace to surrender my choices to You daily as I learn to serve You and love others. Amen.

Read 1 Timothy 6:6-12. How do you choose contentment instead of continually striving toward things that won't satisfy? What does contentment mean to you?

_____

_____

_____

_____

_____

_____

_____

_____

"I had to become a happy single, enthralled with God alone, before God trusted me with a spouse. And though I believed He wanted me married, I still had to choose Jesus every day as the lover of my soul."—*Dawn, 32*

Dateless

He was despised and rejected—a man of
sorrows, acquainted with deepest grief. We
turned our backs on him and looked the other
way. He was despised, and we did not care.

ISAIAH 53:3

What frustrates me most about dating books and chick flicks is that there's always a *love* interest. That was never the case for me growing up! No matter how hard I believed, hoped for, or dreamed about being in a relationship, I was dateless. The hardest part for me was my appearance. I was in junior high when all my health issues began and I started to gain weight. In high school eczema took the skin off my face and feet, and I gained even more weight from the medication. I didn't think anyone would ever love me. It was horrible and depressing. No words of comfort could encourage me to believe again.

It was the summer of my fifteenth birthday that I decided to do something about it. Instead of waiting around for my prince to come, I got into the Word. Daily I studied the Scriptures and it was there that I found hope. I began to realize my worth in Jesus Christ and was affirmed in my identity as His child (John 1:12). Christ became my best friend (John 15:15). Any time I needed to cry or ask God for His help, He was there. My only problem was translating what I saw in the mirror to the boys at school. I realized I wanted someone who truly cared for me and not just for what I looked like.

I realize my story is a bit on the extreme side. After God healed my skin, I lost most of the weight that I had gained from taking medication for eczema. But because of that experience, my self-confidence far surpassed that of even the prettiest girls at the school. I learned not to judge only by appearance. And I learned over time that I could trust God because He too had been rejected. He'd been through pain I'd never experienced. And I trusted that I could rest in Him.

Dear Jesus,

Thank You that I am not alone. Help me to take my hurt and rejection to the foot of the cross to find grace and mercy in my time of need. Amen.

Read Colossians 2:6-10. What if you can't get someone to go out with you? Should you have to change who you are in order to be accepted by a boy or girlfriend?

_____

_____

_____

_____

_____

_____

_____

_____

"I dated someone for nine months before I realized that I had totally changed my personality. Everyone hated who I was becoming and thankfully I dumped him and went back to being my true self. God eventually brought me the perfect guy, who loves me for exactly who I am."—*Stacy, 24*

QUALITY CHARACTER

You can identify them by their fruit, that is, by the
way they act. Can you pick grapes from thornbushes,
or figs from thistles? A good tree produces
good fruit, and a bad tree produces bad fruit.

MATTHEW 7:16-17

Waiting on a promise from God for a future and a hope can take you through many distractions, temptations, and battles of self-will. Do you have what it takes to wait?

Nobody likes to use the *S*-word. Self-control. Solomon said, "A person without self-control is like a city with broken-down walls" (Proverbs 25:28). With your defenses down, you never know what kind of person could weasel into your life. Developing that spiritual muscle of self-control will ensure that only people of quality will come into your "city."

To judge a person's character, ask some basic questions:

1. How does he spend his free time?
2. What kind of friends does she surround herself with?
3. Is he involved in a church group, or does he volunteer anywhere?
4. How has her walk with God grown and developed over the past five years?
5. What does he want his life to look like in five years?

As you ask these questions, you will begin to see behind a person's pretty intentions. In dating, people usually show you the good stuff first, but the good stuff isn't necessarily good fruit. Do your date's actions line up with the words they speak? The Bible is pretty clear: a godly person can't produce bad character, and a bad person can't produce good character.

Spend some time in prayer and in the Word, and trust God to show you the character of the people in your life.

Dear Jesus,

Thank You for giving me the insight to see the true character of the people in my life. Open my eyes to the good in people, and teach me to see them the way You see them. In Your Name, Jesus. Amen.

Read Matthew 7:15-20. What questions do you ask to discern the quality of someone's character?

_____

_____

_____

_____

_____

_____

_____

_____

"Because of the technology that's out there, church, and friends, I could certainly find a relationship if I wanted one. However, that person may not be quality or someone worth truly pursuing. Just because you can doesn't mean you should."—*Richard, 27*

TO DaTe or NOT TO DaTe

Like newborn babies, you must crave pure spiritual
milk so that you will grow into a full experience of
salvation. Cry out for this nourishment, now that
you have had a taste of the Lord's kindness.

1 PETER 2:2-3

Today's question only seems difficult to address because of the culture and world around us. *Seventeen* magazine teaches preteens that they shouldn't be satisfied without a boyfriend, and *Cosmopolitan* markets new articles on relationships, sex, and how to get your man monthly. It's no wonder Christian books have a difficult time addressing the topic of dating and relationships—and staying single. So how do *you* answer this question? With everyone dating around you, is it time for you to get on board?

Of course, you have the *freedom* to go and do as you please. I don't believe it's wrong to date simply to learn more about the opposite sex, but keep the end outcome in mind. If you're not ready for marriage—you're not financially stable, or you parents don't think you're ready—I urge you to be cautious in dating. Once you've crossed a line—be it holding hands, kissing, fooling around, or having sex—it's difficult to go back.

It's easy to be distracted by the fun times and butterflies in dating. But what's the big rush? Maybe you are the only single person in your neighborhood or church. You're tired of watching other people's kids when they go out, and dating seems like the only path to happiness. Or maybe you just want more dating experience. But make sure *your* timing is also *God's* timing. Ask God to show you when you're ready for a relationship!

Dear Jesus,

Sometimes I choose not to listen to You because I don't like the answer. If the answer is "no" or "wait," help me do so joyfully. If the answer is "yes," help me set healthy boundaries in my relationship. Thank You that Your timing is perfect! Amen.

Read Matthew 19:2-12. How will you know when you're ready for marriage? If you're not ready, is it still okay to date?

_____

_____

_____

_____

_____

_____

_____

_____

"When I was in college I knew guys who seemed to spend all their time playing video games. Most of those guys were single. Guys, how important is that Xbox to you?"—*Elliott, 28*

your pride

Pride leads to disgrace, but with
humility comes wisdom.

PROVERBS 11:2

When relationships come to an end, most people are afraid to tell the truth about it. Two hurting people get lost and confused in clichés. "This just isn't working for me." "It's not you; it's me." "I'm not ready for a relationship right now." People avoid the truth for fear of hurting each other, but the lie seems to sting even more.

I did a quick poll online and came up with a pretty lengthy list of the *real* reasons people might end or avoid being in a relationship. Do any of these sound familiar?

- Fear
- Past relationship failures
- Inability to commit
- Not seeing yourself as worthy
- Parent issues
- Self-sabotage
- Not wanting distractions from school, work, or a relationship with Jesus
- Selfishness (unwillingness to give up time, money, etc.)
- Trust issues
- Hidden insecurities

Everyone struggles with their own private issues, many of which will eventually surface in relationships. But no matter which issue you struggle with, C.S. Lewis said, "There is one vice of which no man in the world is free; which every one in the world loathes when he sees it in someone else; and of which hardly any people, except Christians, ever imagine that they are guilty themselves...The essential vice, the utmost evil, is Pride. Unchasity, anger, greed, drunkenness, and all that, are mere fleabites in

132

comparison: it was through Pride that the devil became the devil."* It's no secret that pride is deadly. Examine your motives today and ask God to reveal the lies you've told yourself or others. Strive for honesty and humility—not pride—in all your relationships.

Dear Jesus,

Thank You for uncovering the little white lies I tell myself daily. Don't let me stay the same. Guide my path with Your light, step by step, and help me uncover answers as I seek truth about my relationships. Amen.

Read Psalm 10:12-13. What hidden (or not-so-hidden) sins has God revealed to you? How can you keep them from damaging a relationship (and not just the romantic kind)?

_____

_____

_____

_____

_____

_____

> "I've heard a lot of advice about getting into a relationship, but not so much on why we avoid relationships. I have been single for five years since breaking up with a porn addict, and singleness is easier than having to trust someone."—*Jennie, 29*

---

* C.S. Lewis, *Mere Christianity* (San Francisco, CA: Harper, 2001), 121-22

LETTING GO

A cheerful look brings joy to the heart; good news
makes for good health...A cheerful heart is good
medicine, but a broken spirit saps a person's strength.

PROVERBS 15:30, 17:22

J ust one look, one touch, or one kiss sends you into a place far, far
away where love is easy and trust comes naturally. We all long to be
thought of as worthy. We all want someone to love. Those dreams never
fade—and sometimes they're even more powerful than the reality of real
relationships. People often stay in that dreamy phase of a relationship
much longer than they should, refusing to let go of those tiny little butterflies. Nobody wants to experience abandonment, loneliness, yet another
breakup, or a broken heart smashed into pieces. When a relationship turns
sour it can be deadly to your emotional, physical, and spiritual well-being.

I know many people, including myself, who have let the sting of
unrequited love take them to places they would never imagine *emotionally*. It's not like he wants to be this upset or she wants to cry for days on
end, but it happens. We choose how to react...and yet somehow it feels
as if the choice has been taken from us. Maybe your ex cheated on you, or
said something that you can't forgive—and yet deep down at your core
you still want to. That's what makes it so difficult to let go!

There's nothing worse than the pain of letting go *physically*. We
want closure. We crave human interaction, desperate for a face-to-face
conversation. If you're in the middle of a breakup, keep the golden rule
in mind: "Do to others whatever you would like them to do to you" (Matthew 7:12). It's never okay to break up with someone over Facebook or
text message. Even though it's painful to let go of a person—especially
as it can affect other friendships, the circles you socialize in, and the
places you go—have the integrity to discuss it face-to-face.

The hardest part is when one or both people in the relationship refuse to let go *spiritually*. The Lord has forgiven every one of us way more than "seventy times seven" (Matthew 18:22). When we harbor unforgiveness, we are the ones in danger. Choose to look beyond the hurt, and look forward to a brighter future.

Dear Jesus,

Help me to take responsibility and seek reconciliation in all my broken relationships. Don't let me hold a grudge or seek revenge, but show me a new way forward. Amen.

Read Matthew 18:21-35. How have you been called to forgive?

_____

_____

_____

_____

_____

_____

_____

"My boyfriend and I broke up. He was a great guy, but the distance was killing me and I had some doubts about our compatibility. While it was hard to say good-bye and return to the single life, I am confident I made the right choice and am trusting God to see what he has next."—*Megan, 32*

HOW Far Is Too Far?

But Lot's wife looked back as she was following
behind him, and she turned into a pillar of salt.

GENESIS 19:26

Relationships are not something we can easily walk away from. A friend of mine says, "When we talk about relationships, we are talking about something or someone you don't just walk away from. You always go back. Sometimes you go back to say good-bye, or I'm sorry, or I forgive you." When two people become more than just friends, they now give more of their time, money, and physical affection. I like to set healthy boundaries in all my relationships—not just with my boyfriend. With a significant other, you might draw the line at kissing and holding hands, or just at holding hands. With someone who's just a friend, the line might be even further back.

Once we experience a taste of *the physical*, our affections run wild. The chemicals in our brain release happy endorphins and we crave more. That's why setting those boundaries at the start is so important. Sometimes as Christians (okay! I'll speak for myself here), we get so caught up in wanting to experience the "forbidden fruit" that we're willing to put up with a relationship that is *less* than God's best.

Remember the story of Lot's wife? She and her family were fleeing the destruction of Sodom and Gomorrah. An angel had told them, "Run for your lives! And don't look back or stop anywhere in the valley!" (Genesis 19:17). But as they were running, Lot's wife fell behind and looked back toward her old home. She was turned into a pillar of salt. Just like Lot's wife, we need to remember the commitments we make. When God gives us a command to flee unhealthy people and places, it's our responsibility to go. Far. Running all the way, even though our inclination is to "go back," like my friend said. Even a taste of that forbidden fruit can lead down a dangerous path. As Scripture teachers, "hold on to what is good. Stay away from every kind of evil" (1 Thessalonians 5:21-22).

Dear Jesus,

I ask for Your peace to make me holy in every way, including my relationships. Help me to be found blameless while I wait for Your return. I thank You for making this happen, because You who call me are faithful. Amen.

Read 1 Thessalonians 5:12-24. How far is too far to go in a relationship? What does physical, emotional, or spiritual purity mean to you?

_____

_____

_____

_____

_____

_____

_____

_____

_____

"I've gone too far, and am still struggling with that to
some extent. We each have an emotional line that we
may choose to cross, but in crossing it we blur our vision
of God's line and the purity He calls us to."—*Chris, 29*

THe Inside

I praise you because I am fearfully and wonderfully made; your works are wonderful, I know that full well.

PSALM 139:14 NIV

Everyone has—to some degree—a past they're ashamed of, a future they're afraid of, and a present they have no idea what to do about. Sometimes it can feel as if you hardly know yourself. As a friend of mine puts it, "While it is important to know as much about yourself as possible, there are going to be new things you will discover about yourself in any new relationship, no matter if it's a dating thing, a friend, or a family member."

Have you ever met a guy or a girl and, as you got to know them better over time, they became even *more* attractive? It was because their insides matched their outside. He doesn't just talk about God, but he lives it out by his actions. She doesn't just love God, but loves others as well. Even after you've been in a relationship for a long time, there's still an opportunity to learn more about your significant other. What you find attractive about him or her. Their strengths and weaknesses. And what makes them grow.

When you're showing off your true self in a relationship, it's easier for others to get to know you and it makes God happy! He knows when you sit down and stand up. He knows your thoughts. He knows everything you do and say before you even say it (Psalm 139:1-6). The truth is—you are fearfully and wonderfully made. Inside and out. How do you celebrate your partner?

Dear Jesus,

*Thank You for the ability to make You proud by the way I live
out my relationships. Help me to celebrate my relationships
because we are all created in Your image. Amen.*

Read Psalm 139:1-6. How is the inside more important than what
is on the outside? How can I look for the beauty in another's unique-
ness—or even my own?

_____

_____

_____

_____

_____

_____

_____

_____

"God is concerned with the heart of a person.
Anyone can be cute. Anyone can have a nice face
or bod. But the inside determines the true spirit of
a person. And time will tell that."—*Anna, 27*

TO CHANGE OR
NOT TO CHANGE?

Don't be selfish; don't try to impress others.
Be humble, thinking of others as better than
yourselves. Don't look out only for your own
interests, but take an interest in others, too.

PHILIPPIANS 2:3-4

Did you know your impact could be the catalyst of change in another? Following in the example Christ set for us we learn, "Though he was God, he did not think of equality with God as something to cling to. Instead, he gave up his divine privileges; he took the humble position of a slave and was born as a human being. When he appeared in human form, he humbled himself in obedience to God and died a criminal's death on a cross" (Philippians 2:6-8). Why else do you think Christ commanded us to look to the needs of others—even above our own? When we choose to look to the cross rather than our own circumstances, we find we have everything we need to change our own lives and the hearts of those around us.

While waiting to see change in others, check your own ambitions. Is the change you want for your significant other *selfish*? Christ reminds us, "Do not judge others, and you will not be judged...The standard you use in judging is the standard by which you will be judged" (Matthew 7:1-2). Because I grew up in a legalistic household, I often find myself being harsher on the people I love than I should be. But we shouldn't strive to be better—or make others better—just because we want affirmation from someone else. Here's the real reason for change: "Be kind to each other, tenderhearted, forgiving one another, just as God through Christ has forgiven you" (Ephesians 4:32).

In a relationship, two people are always changing to fit the needs of their partner. Is your significant other willing to work at changing with you? Do the two of you strive to make each other better than you were—and better than you could be on your own? The truth is, we all need a change of heart. But check out what God promises: "I will give them singleness of heart and put a new spirit within them. I will take away their stony, stubborn heart and give them a tender, responsive heart, so they will obey my decrees and regulations. Then they will truly be my people, and I will be their God" (Ezekiel 11:19-20).

Dear Jesus,

Create in me a clean heart, O God. Renew a loyal spirit within me. Surely Your goodness and unfailing love will pursue me all the days of my life. Transform me and help me to grow in a relationship that honors You. Amen.

Read Romans 6:1-4. How have you seen God renewing your mind and spirit? How is He calling you to be a catalyst for change in someone else's life?

_____

_____

_____

_____

_____

_____

"Change has to come from you, so that it becomes second nature."—*Mike, 27*

THE LITTLE THINGS

Catch all the foxes, those little foxes, before they ruin
the vineyard of love, for the grapevines are blossoming.

SONG OF SONGS 2:15

The Song of Songs is a breath of fresh air. The descriptive exchange between the Young Man and his Young Woman captures my heart and my special attention. This erotic poem is spoken between two lovers who celebrate each other with little compliments and grander exclamations of love. They're quite a pair.

What if an outsider read your love story? Would she see a deep, abiding love in Christ? Would she see you learning and growing together in Him? Or rather, would she see a relationship focused on small, petty things that threaten to destroy it? That's the point of today's passage.

Little things matter. In a relationship, commit to paying attention to the little things. Favorite songs, movies, hobbies, food, or even flowers are worth knowing because they show your love in a way that says "I care." Think this little stuff isn't a big deal? Check out the parable that Jesus tells in Matthew 25:14-30. At the end He tells His listeners, "You have been faithful in handling this small amount, so now I will give you many more responsibilities. Let's celebrate together!" (Matthew 25:21).

On the other hand, don't sweat the small stuff. When we focus on the little foxes—the time he forgot to do this, or the time she didn't do that—our small frustrations can easily grow into anger. Ephesians 4:26-27 says, "Don't let the sun go down while you are still angry, for anger gives a foothold to the devil." Resolve to settle your differences quickly, and watch your relationship be all the healthier.

Only one thing matters. Remember the story of Mary and Martha? Martha was busy preparing a meal for Jesus while Mary sat patiently at Jesus's feet, soaking up His presence. I feel for Martha. I really do. She gets a bad rap. Maybe she was having a bad day, and Mary's seeming indifference to her work caused her to fly off the handle. Jesus cut right to Martha's heart. "My dear Martha," He said, "you are worried and upset over all these details! There is only one thing worth being concerned about. Mary has discovered it, and it will not be taken away from her" (Luke 10:41-42).

Dear Jesus,

May we appreciate the wonder that is Your love while learning to celebrate those You bring into our path. Help us to let go of the little things and embrace the one thing that truly matters—You! Amen.

Read Luke 10:38-42. Which little things matter in your relationship? Which little things do you need to let go of?

_____

_____

_____

_____

_____

_____

_____

_____

"Small things matter in a relationship because when they're not done, you can really tell."—*Heidi, 30*

more

My cousin is beautiful, smart, fun, attractive, and godly. Very godly. She graduated from Biola University, got her Master's in Education, and moved to Central America to teach children and serve the poor. She has a heart of gold. So when we started talking about dating I paid extra attention. We discussed the question of godly men and women who aren't attractive by the world's standards. Is it possible, she asked, for attraction to grow? This got me thinking. I have written a lot about guarding your heart, body, and mind. About being careful not to let lust overtake you in a relationship. But what if lust isn't the problem? What if the heart is amazing but you don't feel any attraction?

A solid relationship needs chemistry. I don't mean lust at first date. Nor do I mean similar interests or hobbies. There needs to be a spark between two people in any kind of relationship. *Intimacy matters*. If two people are dating with an eye toward marriage, there should be a level of attraction that will one day lead to greater fulfillment. To two becoming one. Song of Songs 5:9 says, "Why is your lover better than all others, O woman of rare beauty? What makes your lover so special?" Would you be able to answer this question?

Scripture reminds us not to settle for less. There's a story in the Bible about the young king Amaziah. Trusting in man's strength instead of God's, he paid 7,500 pounds of silver to hire 100,000 soldiers. But a man of God told him not to rely on his impressive army for victory. He said, "The LORD is able to give you much more than this!" (2 Chronicles 25:9). *More*. God had something better in mind for Amaziah, and He has the very best in mind for you.

Ancient Greek has several different words for love. The word for

144

passionate, sensual love is *eros*. Eros doesn't have anything to do with a person's physique, haircut, or fashion sense. Instead, it means seeing the beauty inside another person. When you share eros with someone, you see the truth of who God made him or her to be. And what's a big nose or skinny legs in comparison with that?

Dear Jesus,

Help me continue to foster more than my heart, but also my soul and mind for You, Your people, and Your Kingdom. Show me the truth about the people You've brought into my life. Amen.

Read Romans 12:9-10. What does chemistry mean to you? Do you think attraction can grow over time?

_____

_____

_____

_____

_____

_____

"Chemistry and physical attraction matter. Even if a person is 'godly' or has a good heart, you shouldn't pursue a relationship that's not genuine. It's not fair to the other person to lead them on. Being 'godly' is awesome, but there's more to having a real relationship than just that."—*Tim, 27*

WHEN THE GRASS IS GREENER

*Whatever is good and perfect comes down to us
from God our Father, who created all the lights in the
heavens. He never changes or casts a shifting shadow.*

JAMES 1:17

At the end of one of his letters the apostle Paul writes, "Be thankful in all circumstances, for this is God's will for you who belong to Christ Jesus" (1 Thessalonians 5:18). *Gratitude*. No matter what stage of life you're in, you're called to thank God for it. The same goes if you're single or in a relationship. Even when the grass looks greener, we're commanded to praise the Creator for everything He's blessed us with. "The LORD is my shepherd; I have all that I need," says David in Psalm 23:1. *All*. Did you catch that?

Look at the Old Testament. The Israelites had everything they wanted and more—and yet they still grumbled against God. We laugh at their complaints. Poke fun at them. But—and this is a big but—we are just like them. Does this sound familiar? "They [the Israelites] cried out to the LORD, and they said to Moses, 'Why did you bring us out here to die in the wilderness? Weren't there enough graves for us in Egypt? What have you done to us?'...But Moses told the people, 'Don't be afraid. Just stand still and watch the LORD rescue you today." (Exodus 14:10-11,13). Moses had the correct response. Today and every day you have a choice, whether you're faced with the Red Sea of Singleness or you're in a contented relationship. *Be thankful*.

Gratitude is a spiritual muscle that you can build up with time. Grateful now, grateful later. If you practice gratitude as a single person, you'll know how to thank God when you're in a relationship—especially when that relationship has its problems and issues. Jesus commanded us to "Trust in God, and trust also in me" (John 14:1). Trust that God has a purpose for the exact circumstances you're in right now, and trust that even if they're hard, He can use them for your good. Sounds like a good reason to praise Him instead of grumbling like an Israelite!

Dear Jesus,

You are so patient and kind with me. You never rush me, and even when it takes me a while to get it, You're still there with open arms to welcome me back. I confess I haven't been as grateful as I could be lately. Please forgive me and show me how to be thankful today. Amen.

Read Psalm 23. Even if you don't have every blessing—like a spouse or a boyfriend/girlfriend—what other blessings can you thank God for today?

_____

_____

_____

_____

_____

_____

_____

"I have lots of opinions about everything—just ask me! But I don't know what to say about being grateful right now because I'm really not." —*Neal, 27*

AS GOOD AS IT GETS

The blessing of the Lord makes a person
rich, and he adds no sorrow with it.

PROVERBS 10:22

I just watched a video of me speaking at Brick House, the young adult ministry of Potter's House in Dallas, Texas. It was one of the best nights of my life. I was speaking at one of the fastest-growing churches in America, and I had just heard the news that my first book, *Faithbook of Jesus*, had sold out its first print release. I was speaking all across America and I thought—*wow, this is what I've lived for—to tell my story and share about God's redemption. This is as good as it gets.* But as I watch the video, I can see the lies that I still believed.

"I'll never be loved."

That lie still haunts me, even though God has gone out of His way to prove me wrong. It's way too easy to question God's goodness, timing, and intentions towards us. We look around, comparing ourselves to those who are in healthy relationships. We crave knowledge of the future. We want to know when that man or woman of our dreams is going to show up on our doorstep. On that night in Dallas I knew God had fulfilled my professional dreams, but I guess I didn't yet trust Him with my personal desires. I believed the lie that my life was as good as it was going to get.

Check out what one of God's prophets says in Malachi 3:10. In return for our obedience, God promises to "open the windows of heaven for you. I will pour out a blessing so great you won't have enough room to take it in!" *Whoa.* Trust God with all your dreams. Nothing is too big for Him to handle.

Dear Jesus,

Help me remain pure and focused on You while I wait on You to fulfill Your promises in my life. Do not let me be deceived. Thank You that my life is in Your hands—and not the enemy's. Amen.

Read Genesis 3:1-13. Do you believe your life is as good as it gets? What are you currently waiting on God for?

_____

_____

_____

_____

_____

_____

_____

_____

"I used to think my life was as good as it gets, until God did the unthinkable and kept blessing me with the desires of my heart. I have everything I need in Him, and God still continues to bless me."—*Abby, 25*

comfort zone

In the spring of the year, when kings normally go
out to war...David stayed behind in Jerusalem.

2 SAMUEL 11:1

There is nothing wrong with comfort. Comfort food. Eight-foot-long comfy couches. Soft sweaters and real hugs. Not side hugs, but the kind of bear hugs that hurt your rib cage and make you laugh. I love a warm embrace. There are certain people, places, and things that make me feel *instantly* welcome. When I'm in the presence of my family, best friends, or a significant other, they make me want to kick off my flip-flops and stay awhile. I am welcome. *Loved*.

You know you're comfortable in a relationship when you look forward to another person's smell, laugh, and little idiosyncrasies. There's nothing wrong with comfort, but it's when life is going great that we have to be the most careful. "If you think you are standing strong, be careful not to fall," warns Paul in 1 Corinthians 10:12. Makes sense, but what does this look like?

David stayed comfortably in his palace when he should have been going off to war. Because of his idleness, he fell into sin with Bathsheba—a sin that culminated in the murder of her husband. At a time in my life when I was "comfortable" in a job, I didn't see the harm in flirting with a cute guy at work. Instead of finding my comfort in Christ I let my anxiety push me into the arms of a man I barely knew. As the harmless flirtation grew more serious, I came to understand that I needed to say *no* to sin and *yes* to God. I ended the relationship, finished my degree with such fervor, moved out of my parents' house, landed my dream job, and published my first book. What about you? What kind of godly sorrow has God used in your life to move you out of your comfort zone?

Dear Jesus,

Thank You for moving me beyond the comfortable and placing me back in Your loving arms. Don't let me be afraid of godly sorrow, for that is where I will find hope, healing, and the truth of Your promises. Amen.

Read 2 Corinthians 7:10-12. Has God ever knocked you out of your comfort zone? What was the result and what did you end up doing about it?

_____

_____

_____

_____

_____

_____

_____

_____

"It is possible to get too comfortable in your relationships
if either person stops seeking God's wisdom and
begins to rely completely on their partner. I've had
it happen to me. I began to seek a friend's council
instead of taking my burdens to the cross and
leaving them in God's hands."—*Jessica, 23*

LET'S TALK ABOUT...TALKING!

Let the wise listen to these proverbs and become even
wiser. Let those with understanding receive guidance.

PROVERBS 1:5

Let's face it: in our relationships, we don't always put in the face time
that we should. We don't communicate and talk about the big issues
until it's almost too late. Is your prayer life like that? We thank God for
a meal, a good day's work, and Friday (especially if it's a pay day). But
our prayers change when life gets tough. All of a sudden we pray like
crazy—right? If you've been in touch with God about the big stuff all
along, though, the tough times are a lot easier to handle.

Effective prayer gets us through life just like communication guides
a relationship. Whenever I find one of my relationships struggling, I
keep open lines of communication and strive to share my heart—and
the heart of God—with the other person. Here are four keys to keeping
effective and godly communication alive and well in your relationships:

1. *Seek Him now!* "Plant the good seeds of righteousness, and you will harvest a crop of love. Plow up the
   hard ground of your hearts, for now is the time to seek
   the LORD, that he may come and shower righteousness upon you" (Hosea 10:12).

2. *Tackle tough issues together.* "Then if my people who
   are called by my name will humble themselves and
   pray and seek my face and turn from their wicked
   ways, I will hear from heaven and will forgive their
   sins and restore their land" (2 Chronicles 7:14).

3. *Seek wise counsel.* "When the Father sends the
   Advocate as my representative—that is, the Holy

Spirit—he will teach you everything and will remind you of everything I have told you" (John 14:26).

4. *Press for His blessings.* "Oh, that we might know the LORD! Let us press on to know him. He will respond to us as surely as the arrival of dawn or the coming of rains in early spring" (Hosea 6:3).

Dear Jesus,

Thank You for giving us Your Holy Spirit to help us communicate with You and others. Don't let me sin by letting anger gain control of me. Give me the strength to fight for my relationships today! Amen.

Read James 3:1-12. How do you communicate in a relationship? What if you have different styles of communicating? How can you ensure effective communication?

_____

_____

_____

_____

_____

_____

"It's important to understand and accept your differences in communication. As a healthy relationship progresses each person must be willing to adjust a little. But most of all, it's important just to communicate!"—*Missy, 28*

THE POWER OF PRAYER

The earnest prayer of a righteous person has
great power and produces wonderful results.

JAMES 5:16

Prayer is powerful. Through prayer, we have direct access to God and the power of His Spirit. In Hebrews 4:16, we're instructed to "come boldly to the throne of our gracious God. There we will receive his mercy, and we will find grace to help us when we need it most." One of the most heartfelt prayers in the Bible concerning a future spouse is found in Genesis 24:12-14. Abraham's servant was praying to find a wife for his master's son Isaac. It's the verse after that shows the power of prayer. "Before he had finished praying, he saw a young woman named Rebekah coming out with her water jug on her shoulder" (verse 15). Abraham's servant asked God if this woman was the answer to his prayer. *She was!* He then "bowed low and worshipped the Lord" (verse 26).

When was the last time you gave thanks to God for answering your prayers?

God doesn't always show us the answer to prayer immediately, as he did for Isaac and Rebekah. But that doesn't mean God is mean, aloof, or inconsiderate. Our response to unanswered prayer is to wait and learn. God is always teaching us if we're willing to listen. Sometimes He teaches us accountability. Will we be faithful to our future spouse even when we can't see him or her yet? God wants us to rely on His ways in His timing—not ours. Isaiah 55:8-9 reminds us, "'My thoughts are nothing like your thoughts,' says the LORD. 'And my ways are far beyond anything you could imagine. For just as the heavens are higher than the earth, so my ways are higher than your ways and my thoughts higher than your thoughts.'" Often times, we do a horrible job of making decisions on mundane things that don't even matter. How much more important is it to rely on the power of prayer for our future spouse?

Prayer brings the hidden things to light (Mark 4:22). Let God work in you, transforming you and your future spouse so that you will both be whole when you finally come together. And while you're waiting on your better half, remember to pray without ceasing. "And Isaac brought Rebekah into his mother Sarah's tent, and she became his wife. He loved her deeply, and she was a special comfort to him after the death of his mother" (Genesis 24:67).

Dear Jesus,

It's a great day to pray and seek Your will regarding my relationships. Help me to rejoice in confident hope, be patient in trouble, and keep on praying for my future spouse. Keep him/ her safe and bring us together in Your timing. Amen.

Read Genesis 24:12-27. Write a prayer for your future spouse below.

_____

_____

_____

_____

_____

"I pray for my future spouse in general, and specifically things like success at her job, a continuing and deepening walk with Christ, and that God would lead her to me, as the way I see it, I'm made for her as much as she is made for me."—*Loren, 29*

LOYALTY PAINS

When the Lord saw that Leah was unloved,
he enabled her to have children.

GENESIS 29:31

Loyalty. It hurts when someone leaves, breaks up, or cheats on you. It hurts beyond words. Misery loves company, and that's why God asks us to get connected. We're here to encourage one another. Take long walks. Talk and share. Pray together and point each other back to God—even when He is silent.

Leah is the best biblical example of this. She was not loved. Nor was she the favorite wife of Jacob. After Leah's father tricked Jacob into marrying her, Jacob spent seven years working for the hand of her younger sister, Rachel. Ouch. Talk about a loyal pain. But the Lord noticed her misery. As Ann Spangler and Jean Syswerda put it, "The God of Abraham, Isaac, and Jacob (Leah's husband) looked down and saw a woman who was lonely and sad because her husband loved his other wife better than he loved her. So, to ease her sorrow, to provide her comfort, God gave her children—beautiful, upright, strong children, one of whom would found the lineage of the priests of Israel and another who was an ancestor of Jesus Himself."*

I know some of you—myself included—have experienced deep sorrow from a painful breakup. From someone breaking his or her commitment. Maybe you're the one who broke it. You never know how God's going to redeem your love story. He's still writing the pages as we speak. Learn to trust Him and put your hand in His. He'll lead you down the path of righteousness. Next time you're tempted to believe you're the only one with heartache in relationships, take heart and think again.

---

* Ann Spangler and Jean E. Syswerda, *Women of the Bible* (Grand Rapids, MI: Zondervan, 1999), 69.

Since the time of Genesis God has been making and remaking His covenant to His people. Unlike your ex, "God is not a man, so he does not lie. He is not human, so he does not change his mind. Has he ever spoken and failed to act? Has he ever promised and not carried it through?" (Numbers 23:19). No. Say it again: No! No loyalty pains or broken commitments can separate you from God's love.

Dear Jesus,

I am convinced that neither death nor life, angels nor demons, fears from the past nor present worries can separate us from You. Be our shield in times of distress. Come to our aid and rescue us in our brokenness. Amen.

Read Jeremiah 31:3-4. How do you keep your commitments? How does God want you to act towards those who didn't keep his or her commitments to you?

_____

_____

_____

_____

_____

"I forgive the first few times, but if they keep breaking
their word and doing hurtful things I get angry and
anger makes me pull away, using distance to protect
myself. I had to learn to manage my anger as a
newlywed: it was either drama queen, pit bull, or cold
shoulder—none are good choices. "—*Pam Farrel*

AND...ACTION!

Watch what God does, and then you do it, like children
who learn proper behavior from their parents.

EPHESIANS 5:1 MSG

When I tried online dating I noticed that almost everyone and their brother listed their religious beliefs as "Christian." God calls us not to judge, but...really? I went on a few blind dates with guys that claimed to be believers. Why did some of them press me to sleep with them? Christ calls us to stay pure and act like proper children. I'm not saying it's easy to do. Thankfully, I have Christ-like parents who have taken a vested interest in my love life. Every time I go out on dates they always ask me if I was pure. It's an awkward conversation to have with your mother, but I thank God for her concern. If she didn't keep me accountable and set a godly example for me, I might have fallen into sin long ago.

My faith—at some point—had to become my own. I made decisions not based on my parents' happiness or pleasing them—but because I wanted to please God and serve Him. The New Living Translation of today's passage and the verses that follow says, "Imitate God, therefore, in everything you do, because you are his dear children. Live a life filled with love, following the example of Christ...Let there be no sexual immorality, impurity, or greed among you. Such sins have no place among God's people."

Why are these instructions so hard to keep? Why are there millions of Christians masquerading as children of light—when they are actually acting in darkness? "So we are lying if we say we have fellowship with God but go on living in spiritual darkness; we are not practicing the truth" (1 John 1:6). And...*action*! If you went on a blind date tonight, how would your date be able to tell if you were a Christian? How do you imitate Christ with your actions—whether you're in a relationship or not?

AND...ACTION!

Dear Jesus,

Thank You for calling me Your child. Help me to live to please You and not myself or my parents—no matter how good their intentions towards me. I ask for help to imitate You in everything I do and say. Amen.

Read 1 John 1:5-10. What does it look like to imitate Christ with your actions? Who do you turn to for support? What is one thing you can do today to change the perception of "hypocrite" Christianity?

_____

_____

_____

_____

_____

_____

_____

_____

"I think the hardest part of dating after being saved was the guilt I felt and the struggles I dealt with trying to follow God and redefine lines that had already been crossed in my current relationship. I found this struggle overwhelming and I felt like I had no one to turn to who would guide me and direct me to make the right, healthy choices." —*Ronel, 31*

159

Jesus, take the lead

Then Elimelech died, and Naomi was left with her
two sons. The two sons married Moabite women.
One married a woman named Orpah, and the
other a woman named Ruth. But about ten years
later, both Mahlon and Kilion died. This left Naomi
alone, without her two sons or her husband.

RUTH 1:3-5

The best sermon I ever heard on dating came from Pastor Mark
Driscoll in his study of Ruth. Driscoll presented Ruth in a light I'd
never heard before—from the perspective of a single Christian male. He
said, "Some of you men have a mental or an actual list of what you're
looking for in a wife. How many of you'd include pagan family, most of
her life spent in a cult, homeless, flat broke, pitted out, dirty, with a crazy,
angry mother-in-law as a bonus prize?"* Flaws. Ruth had plenty of them.
I have them. So do you. We're all wounded and broken, and our lives are
far from perfect. We can't see the next step forward. We think our past
keeps us from having God's best. We wonder how God could ever use us.

That's certainly how Ruth felt. She was a grieving widow. She was
broke, relying on the kindness of strangers just to get a meal. At times,
she must have wanted to fall into despair. But she had one thing that
trumped all of that: faith. She trusted God to direct her life, and she
put Him in charge. She let Him take the lead on everything from her
finances to her love life. And check out what happens in return for her
obedience: after all her grief, Ruth married a man named Boaz and had a
son who became a direct ancestor of Jesus Christ, the Messiah. Who's to
say God can't use broken people? Let God take the lead in your life, and
wait for Him to work His wonders. Lead me Lord, I'm waiting!

---

* Mark Driscoll, "Redeeming Ruth Part 2: God's Hand in Our Luck" (sermon, Mars Hill Church, Seattle, WA, January 14, 2007).

Dear Jesus,

Where You lead I will follow. Help me take courage in my strengths and give my weaknesses to You. Show me what they are so I can move away from my broken past and into the glory You've planned for me. Amen.

Read Exodus 3:1-16. Is it easy to follow God's leading? Why or why not? How do you lead or follow in your relationships?

_____

_____

_____

_____

_____

_____

_____

_____

"In every definition dating is leading on, but that is part of finding love. You don't date just to date, but you do take a chance when you're ready for marriage. You give it to God and you take risks. God uses men who take risks." —*Mark, 28*

BrIDesmaIDs

Then the Kingdom of Heaven will be like
ten bridesmaids who took their lamps and
went to meet the bridegroom. Five of them
were foolish, and five were wise.

MATTHEW 25:1-2

The time to play at work is when the boss leaves on vacation. That's when you get away with talking on the phone, checking e-mail, and posting on Facebook, right? Or if Mr. or Ms. Right hasn't appeared on the horizon...well, what's the problem with fooling around with someone who *is* available? No one's watching, right?

Even though God allows U-turns, there are consequences for sin. Jesus tells a story about this in Matthew 25:1-13. The Parable of the Ten Bridesmaids has haunted me for the past few weeks. In the story, ten bridesmaids were waiting for the bridegroom. Five took extra oil for their lamps, but the others thought they'd have enough. The bridegroom was delayed, and the oil began to run out. The "foolish" bridesmaids left to buy more, and the bridegroom came while they were gone. They missed out on the wedding feast because they hadn't prepared for his arrival.

Please hear my heart in this. I know a lot of us have made foolish decisions. One time too many. And now you feel stuck, locked out of that wedding feast. No longer worthy of human love. No longer worthy of God's love.

But God offers forgiveness. He offers grace. And He blesses the relationships He finds waiting and watching in purity. You can trust Him today and every day! Make God your focus, the Kingdom your work, and all your relationships will succeed.

Dear Jesus,

Let me be found faithful so that, at the appropriate time, You can bring me together with the man/woman of my dreams. I thank You that You can do more for me than I ever think or imagine. In Jesus's precious and Holy name, Amen.

Read Matthew 25:1-13. How do you spend your time waiting?

_____

_____

_____

_____

_____

_____

_____

_____

"I knew my husband was the one because he didn't play games. He wanted to spend time with me more than anyone else."—*Kristie, 22*

Plans

You will keep in perfect peace all who trust in
you, all whose thoughts are fixed on you!

ISAIAH 26:3

I'm very good at making plans. I was going to graduate from college, get married, and have babies. Oops...okay, so that didn't happen. So I landed my dream job and was going to make it my full-time career. Um... apparently that wasn't in the plan either!

Proverbs 16:9 says, "We can make our plans, but the LORD determines our steps." No matter what ideas I have about my future, the only thing I can count on is being *surprised*. The Lord promises a ripe future for those who trust in Him. We can't always know where that future will take us, but we can rest in the assurance that it will be a thousand times better than anything we could plan for ourselves! Here's one of my favorite promises: "And I am certain that God, who began the good work within you, will continue his work until it is finally finished on the day when Christ Jesus returns" (Philippians 1:6). There are two great hopes in this promise. First, we know that God has already begun to work out His plans. You can see it in your life—how He has used "unimportant" people and events to draw you closer to Him! Second, we know that the work *isn't finished*. God has more to show us, and more work for us to do in the kingdom. No matter how frustrated we may be, no matter how lonely, we can proceed in the assurance that our story isn't over. We can't plan the ending, and the plot seems twisted and confused along the way, but we know that God has something spectacular in store! "'For I know the plans I have for you,' says the LORD. 'They are plans for good and not for disaster, to give you a future and a hope'" (Jeremiah 29:11).

We don't need to fear, no matter how confusing and complex our relationships may appear. God knows when, who, and how. Praise God that He is the author of love, the giver of all perfect gifts, and the desire of our hearts. Return to God and rest in Him, waiting on the abundant surprise He has in store for you.

Dear Jesus,
   I am confident of Your faithfulness, and confident that in all things You're working for my good. I praise You for Your mercy, Lord. Keep me strong as I wait on Your surprise! Amen.

Read Psalm 71. Write God a heartfelt prayer, asking for His guidance and praising Him for the many blessings He has already bestowed.

_____

_____

_____

_____

_____

_____

_____

_____

"I'm currently single and am striving to be content, but would rather be in a relationship."—*Nathan, 28*

connect with the author

Renee Fisher is a spirited speaker and writer to twenty-somethings. She graduated from Biola University and worked with nationally known Christian speakers and writers at Outreach Events. Her devotional blog reaches hundreds of readers. Renee's mission in life is to "spur others forward" (Hebrews 10:24) using the lessons learned from her own trials to encourage others in their walk with God. Learn more about Renee at www.devotionaldiva.com.

Please join the community to share about your dating and relationship stories of heartbreak to happy endings at http://www.notanotherdatingbook.com or connect with Renee on:

Twitter: http://www.twitter.com/devotionaldiva

Facebook: http://www.facebook.com/devotionaldiva

Blog/Web: http://www.devotionaldiva.com

OTHER HARVEST HOUSE BOOKS YOU MAY ENJOY

God's Heart for You —*Holley Gerth*

Popular writer and counselor Holley Gerth invites women to the inspiration and delight of devotions, reflective questions, and captivating poetry that reveal how, through God's love, they are wholly accepted, empowered, and known. This hardcover is a powerful treasury of God's heart and purpose for women.

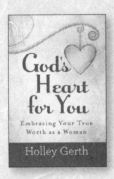

12 Questions to Ask Before You Marry —*Clayton and Charie King*

Longing to help dating couples prepare for lasting marriages, popular author and pastor Clayton King and his wife, Charie, guide them through 12 relationship-building questions about family, finances, and faith and unveil the biblical perspective that creates a forever marriage—it is better to serve rather than be served.

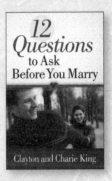

The 10 Best Decisions a Single Can Make —*Bill and Pam Farrel*

Bill and Pam Farrel, bestselling authors of *The 10 Best Decisions a Couple Can Make*, now lead single men and women through the ten most influential decisions they can make to experience faith, fulfillment, and purpose. This encouraging, biblical guide helps readers embrace God's heart and plan for them.

Sassy, Single, and Satisfied
—Michelle McKinney Hammond

Bestselling author Michelle McKinney Hammond encourages singles to use their unique opportunities to be gifts to the world. Always upbeat, always biblical, Michelle reveals how to find joy now, including getting fit spiritually and emotionally. Lively stories reveal how to find contentment, prepare for mates, and revel in God's love.

Single-Minded Devotion
—Michelle McKinney Hammond

Creative, dynamic devotions help singles focus on life's joys, their relationship with God, and discovering solutions to everyday issues, including longing for love. Drawing on biblical moments and encounters with God, Michelle encourages readers to embrace life and answer God's call. Over 275 readings offer thought-provoking insights and practical applications.

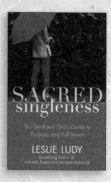

Sacred Singleness *—Leslie Ludy*

Popular speaker and author, Leslie Ludy, shares a powerful message for today's single young women. You can live a passionate, fulfilling life right now rather than one of constantly striving to find the "right one." Firsthand stories and testimonials of modern-day single women will help readers find delight, purpose, and true joy in their lives.

To learn more about books by Renee Fisher or
to read sample chapters, log on to our website:

www.harvesthousepublishers.com

HARVEST HOUSE PUBLISHERS
EUGENE, OREGON